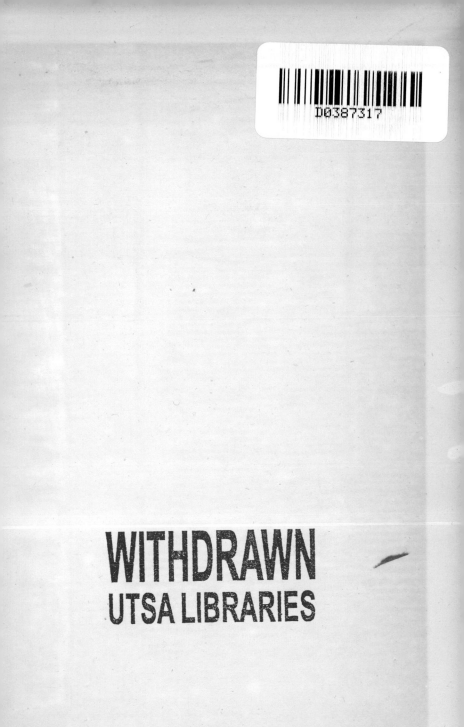

MUSIC AT BELMONT

MUSIC

AT

BELMONT

AND OTHER ESSAYS
AND ADDRESSES

J. T. SHEPPARD

Provost of King's College, Cambridge

RUPERT HART-DAVIS
SOHO SQUARE LONDON
1951

TO FRIENDS AT YALE
IN GRATEFUL MEMORY
OF KINDNESS UNFORGETTABLE

Printed in Great Britain by Butler & Tanner Ltd., Frome and London

ACKNOWLEDGMENTS

To my friends, the publishers, I am grateful for suggesting this attempt to gather in a book these talks on Greek and English poetry, and for the patient kindness and advice which have made the task a pleasure. To Dr. John Masefield, O.M., and the Society of Authors I owe special thanks for allowing me to quote a passage which has cheered and helped me, from his poem "Wonderings"; to Mr. Cecil Day Lewis and Messrs. Jonathan Cape for permitting me to use a passage from his admirable book on the Poetic Image; to the Clarendon Press, Oxford, for the use of lines from *The Testament of Beauty* by Robert Bridges; to Lady Raleigh and Messrs. Methuen for an extract from a letter by Sir Walter Raleigh, and to Captain H. M. Raleigh and Messrs. Constable for some lines from his "Ode to the Glasgow Ballad Club"; to the Macmillan Company for some lines from Thomas Hardy's poem "Surview." For permission to reprint my Presidential Address of 1943 I am indebted to the Council of the Classical Association, and also for the use of passages from my article, "Helen with Priam" in *Greece and Rome*; for the like courtesy to the Royal Institution for my essay on *Milton's*

Cambridge Exercises, and to the Royal Society of Literature for the substance of my essay on *Athens, A Garden of the Muses*. Mr. Arnold Lunn has kindly allowed me to use parts of a version from Hesiod which I made for the Hellenic Travellers' Club in 1926, and occasionally I have used material from talks which I have given in the Third Programme of the B.B.C. Last but not least my friends in the Classical Society at Harvard and the Aurelian Society and Elizabethan Club at Yale may well think, if they do me the honour of reading this book, that there was truth in the remark of a Cambridge (England) undergraduate—"It doesn't matter what title you announce. It's always the same lecture."

Above all I am deeply grateful to those friends at Yale who gave me the privilege of speaking, as Hoyt Lecturer for 1948, some words in memory of one who loved Yale well and is beloved there still, James Humphry Hoyt, a scholar and an athlete of singularly gracious personality, who died in the first promise of his youth. The essay on *The Muses and the Gift of Happiness* is part of the talk I gave in memory of him.

CONTENTS

THE RELEVANCE OF GREEK POETRY   9

HELICON: THE MUSES AND THEIR PUPIL   33

THE NOD OF ZEUS   44

THE SCAEAN GATE   69

THE HOMECOMING TO ITHACA   95

ATHENS, A GARDEN OF THE MUSES   106

MUSIC AT BELMONT   129

MILTON'S CAMBRIDGE EXERCISES   152

THE PRESIDENT OF THE IMMORTALS   163

THE CHARIOTEER   179

THE MUSES AND THE GIFT OF HAPPINESS   187

THE RELEVANCE
OF GREEK POETRY

A PRESIDENTIAL ADDRESS DELIVERED
TO THE CLASSICAL ASSOCIATION IN THE
REGENT HOUSE AT CAMBRIDGE

THIS Regent House was once the Chapel of the University of Cambridge. Meeting in such a place, we are reminded that our ancient schools and colleges were built, as Arthur Gray, who knew and loved their history, has said, "for the Divinity which in our speech we call Knowledge, but to our thoughts it is something holier."

Holier than Knowledge? What Divinity is this? Shall we say Truth? Or, rather, since Truth is still veiled and we are human, shall we say Wisdom, ἁγία Σοφία?

Wisdom is wont to walk with Freedom, child of Courage; with Honesty of mind and heart, and with the love of Beauty: with Justice also, whom we mortals often seek in tears, sometimes with broken hearts: and yet, when a child smiles or a bird sings, Happiness, we know, may come again, with

> Laughter learnt of friend
> In hearts at peace . . .

Wisdom indeed is best sought in the company

9

of friends, *Amicus Plato, magis amica Veritas* is good. But the Socratic formula is better: "I turn over and peruse with my friends the treasures that wise men have written in their books and left us. If we see anything good, we gather it, and we count it a great gain if in so doing we make friends with one another." [1]

Freedom and human Friendship—these are the true divinities of English poetry and of English education at its best. But they were first revealed to poets under the clear skies of Hellas, where they are still honoured by the lives and in the hearts of simple men and women, who, like Homer's heroes, still, in spite of all, use only one and the same word for "stranger," "foreigner," and "guest." [2]

Long ago a Greek lay, naked, buffeted and bruised and helpless, under heaped-up leaves among the bushes by a river. He was near death, but he was Odysseus still. He was like the spark of fire a careful rustic covers with ash at night that it may live till morning. With the dawn came lovely maidens to the meadow, washed their clothes, then played their game of ball. They were the mothers of the race which taught us to play games for fun. The Greeks called education play. Their school was leisure. One of the girls threw badly, and the ball fell into the stream. We know the story. But have we noticed what Odysseus said when he was wakened by their cry? "Ah me,

[1] Xenophon, *Memorabilia*, I. vi, 14.
[2] A. A. Matsas, *Contemporary Poetry and Drama in Greece*, p. 3.

what sort of people live here? Are they savage, arrogant and cruel, and unjust? Or are they friends to strangers, men of a god-fearing mind?" [1]

The secret of the miracle of Greece is in that sentence. It was through faith in the pursuit of wisdom, justice, human kindness, that Homer educated Greece, and Greece, with Rome and Palestine, the modern world.

To-day, when nerves are jangled and minds dazed both by the tragedy of war and by the shock of the discovery that science has, for good and evil, brought a revolution in material conditions, we need not wonder that harsh voices cry "Scrap old ideas." Some indeed we shall do well to scrap, but not the best gifts of our heritage.

The Muses are immortal, and you cannot scrap them. As Saintsbury said, "If you try to scrap what is permanent, it may scrap you." [2]

Nevertheless, we may ignore them, at our peril, or unwittingly lose sight of them. That is the danger. That is why we must be vigilant. Year after year, for many years, in schools and colleges, less and less Greek has been available, and lately, year by year, less and less Latin. Yet we know that, without vital contact with the ancient sources of our inspiration, and some knowledge of the ways in which our liberties were won, we cannot understand the past or wisely serve the future. Many of our colleagues, men of science and affairs as well as men of letters, see the danger

---

[1] *Od.* vi, 119 ff.   [2] *Collected Essays*, vol. iii, p. 341.

too. Therefore I hope that, when we gird on controversial armour and defend the classics, as the men of Corpus Christi College, Oxford, always valiant, did in 1519, controversy will not end in riots, led on both sides by the clergy, as it did in those brave days. We shall do well to remember Henry the Eighth's Fool, who when he found the King transported with unusual joy because the Pope had styled him the Defender of the Faith, "Oh good Harry," quoth the Fool, "let thou and I defend each other, and let the Faith alone to defend itself." [1]

Let the Muses alone to sing. They have been singing since the Sons of the Morning sang together. But the children cannot hear them, and we cannot hear them, unless spirits are attuned. To interrupt is easy. It isn't so easy to help. We mustn't let our wrangling make it difficult for boys and girls to listen. They want to hear the music, once they get the chance. The quality of their reception varies with the instrument with which they came into the world. Some have better dynamos than others. But much depends for all of them on tuning in to the right wavelength and on keeping the good dynamo alive. And that depends, in part at least, on us.

We shall need modesty and patience, if we are to help. A friend of mine, a splendid singer, sang to a village audience some of the sort of songs which, I suppose, most trained musicians would

[1] Fuller, *Church-History of Britain*, v, p. 23.

enjoy. A rustic hearer told him frankly, "You sing muck! Why do you sing muck?" My friend made no defence, but asked, "What sort of songs do *you* like?" "Hymns, like this:

> When upon life's ocean you are tempest-tossed,
> When you are down-hearted and you think all's lost,
> Count your many blessings, count them one by one,
> And it will surprise you what the Lord has done."

Smile a little, as that other old song says. By all means smile. But don't, for goodness' sake—for the sake of his goodness and of your own hopes of goodness—don't let the smile be discouraging. He may not yet have tuned in, but the dynamo is working. Try him again with Handel. Some day you may hear him when the saints with reclad voices chant their Hallelujah, while a hundred messengers and ministers of life eternal sing together *Benedictus qui venit*, strewing flowers above and below—*Manibus date lilia plenis*.

That rustic critic knew the difference between muck and flowers, although he hadn't had much chance. What if he had been a town-boy, from the potteries or "special areas"? His wits might have been sharper, and he more difficult to help. What if he knew no songs except a song of sixpence? What if he had been told, there's nothing real except what can be calculated, measured, rationed?

My own experience was different, but perhaps not quite irrelevant. I was a town-boy, and my parents not well off. I was a late developer, and since, until I was about sixteen, whatever little promise did appear was mathematical, in these days almost certainly I should have had no Greek, and very little Latin.

And yet I knew quite soon I wanted Greek. How did I know? Thanks to a Mr. Robinson of Balliol, who kept a little private school, of a kind disappearing fast to-day under the wheels of "progress." Next to my parents and a bookshop (are there bookshops now in Rye Lane, Peckham?) I owe gratitude to him. He taught us Latin, Euclid, English History and Shakespeare—he made us act and asked no questions, so we loved it. On his desk he kept a big book open which he seemed to like much better than the grammar. He could read it and we couldn't. It was printed in strange characters, rather attractive, I thought.

One day Miss Ramsden, the lady who taught catechism—I wasn't allowed to do that because my parents were Baptists: the result was that I classed it with the works of Byron and with *Pride and Prejudice*, which mother also banned—Miss Ramsden told me to go up to the Headmaster and ask him for the poker. I was small, and I said, "Please, sir, please, sir," timidly, "Please, may I have the poker?" "Yes, little boy, if you won't be afraid," a gruff voice answered, and it changed the world. "Please, sir, please, sir, what's that book?" "Brave! Greek!" Greece has never given him the lie.

When I went to Dulwich, I was asked, "German or Greek?" Of course I said "Greek." When I got home, mother told me, "You ought to have said German. Much more useful." But mother was kind and wise, and I did Greek.

Thanks to that blessed little school I knew some Latin, and at Dulwich, where our teachers were no pedants, after one term, or at most two, of easy exercises came the *Odyssey*. The die was cast, and I was happy.

All children love the *Odyssey* and most of them enjoy it much more if we give them just enough Greek to discern the music when they read it in Greek with a crib. That is enough. They will enjoy it. Some will ask for more. A few will become scholars.

This, after all, may be our best, our one irrefutable argument. What Greek has given us, it can give others—happiness and fun, in hearts, if not at peace, at least not utterly bewildered and afraid. We have been fortunate. We want to share our luck. We want to give a chance to other girls and boys who would enjoy it, rich or poor, country or town, clever or not so clever—late developers, for instance, whom in our certificated blindness we too often class as stupid. Can we not do it somehow? Shall Gloucester lads no longer walk in Hellas,

> And ponder how from Attic seed
> There grew an English tree,
> How Byron, like his heroes, fell,
> Fighting a country free?

Can we not give the children equal opportunity of access to these treasures? That is all we ask for them. No more. No less.

"Be brave," Athena said to young Telemachus. "Are you your father's son?" "My mother says so." "You won't be a nameless nobody if you are her son?" [1] "Be a man," she said. "Some things you will think of for yourself, and some a god will put into your heart."

To Odysseus she said, "I cannot leave you, though you are unfortunate, because you have a gift of speech, quick wits, and a stout loyal heart."

He was like a father to his people, and the swineherd loved him. So did the dog Argos. So did I.

But I admired the Cricket Captain even more. It was delightful when a big boy went up to Odysseus and said, "Sir, you don't look like an athlete—more like a merchant—but would you care to have a try?" and when Odysseus said, "The gods don't give all their good gifts to any one of us. You, my lad, are handsome, but they haven't given you the brains." And I was happy when that boy apologized so handsomely.

But it was better still when the minstrel's voice was hushed in the shadowy hall, and even the suitors were silent, for Penelope stood before them, veiled and weeping.

Then the *Iliad*, that tale of the youth who cared so much for glory and success, but found that

[1] *Od.* i, 206 ff.; iii, 26 f.; xiii, 331; viii, 159 ff.; i, 337 ff.

friendship mattered more, and of the hero fighting for a cause he knew was lost, and of his wife, awaiting his return, and heating a warm bath to welcome him.

A lad who fought in the war of 1914 told me he was stunned once by a shell, and when he woke he was in a hot bath, and a kind nurse bathing his head. At school a master had told him that in Greek they said "warm washings" when we say "a bath." When he saw the nurse he said, "Now I know how Hector felt."

Such things matter. Next, Euripides, begun in the middle of the term in a new form, and so in the middle of a play. The first lines of Greek Tragedy I construed were from Hecuba again, grieving yet comforted: [1]

> And this that they have told me—though I weep:
> I cannot so forget as not to weep—
> Yet you have robbed grief of its sting, because
> They tell me, you were noble. . . . This is strange. . . .
> And what's the reason? Is it birth or breeding?
> Certainly to be bred in a good habit
> Gives them a standard, teaches them a rule
> By which to judge what's base.

One didn't at the time quite realize. And the master's comment was astringent—"Euripides *will* philosophize." But it all helped.

Then the delight of Aristophanes. Aeschylus and Sophocles came later. Pindar, at school, I could not understand. But I liked this, "The sun

---

[1] Euripides, *Hecuba*, 589 ff.

shines for them when it is night here, and their
suburb is in meadows where red roses bloom." [1]

In England, when the Regent House was
built at Cambridge, we were emerging from an
age of strife and poverty and disappointment.
Rotheram, who built the room for us, was one
of the first fellows of King Henry's College. He
was dead before the work was done—about 1500.
And a little way from here the bare walls of a
roofless chapel seemed to prove the Royal Saint's
design a folly. Let me say at once, the education
given in our medieval University was "efficient,"
for the sharpening of wits. It was what some
"educationalists" pray for—strictly and success-
fully "vocational." It turned out prelates, lawyers
and administrators, well equipped to make their
way—but whither? Some were saints, some
scoundrels, most of them, like Rotheram and you
and me, a mixture. But it was too dry, too logical,
too abstract, too much divorced from human
interests and from kindness to justify our claim—
our prayer—*Hinc lucem et pocula sacra*. We had
become estranged from the Muses.

We hadn't always been strangers. Chaucer and
his pilgrims knew them, though they had no
Greek. Why? The poetry of Israel, the Psalms,
the Gospels and the stories of the Saints still
cheered and heartened them. Alas, is it so with us?
It kept some of them a bit straighter than they

[1] Fr. 129 (Bergk.).

18

might have been, and kept them all alive and merry . . . nearly all of them. Why? Some strains and echoes of the classical renaissance had come to them from Italy and France. That helped. Partly it was that they were English, and our character, that inconsistent, lovable, exasperating product of our Anglo-Roman, Anglo-Saxon, Anglo-Norman, Anglo-Scottish origin (Anglo-Catholic in the true sense), our climate and our ways of town and country life *in those days* made us what we were. . . . And what we are? I hope so. But we have a responsibility. There *was* a dark age after Chaucer . . . then this happened. . . .

The Muses weren't dead. They had never deserted. But they were much more likely to be met on the road or in a tavern than at church or in a schoolroom, more likely almost anywhere than in a Cambridge lecture-room. Then the dawn came thus. The Lady Margaret and her confessor Fisher founded a Professorship and Preachership, not to promote the study of the classics, but to teach young parsons how to read the Vulgate not too stupidly, and how to feed the flock with honest, whole-meal sermons, not with husks of logic. That was enough. A new age had begun.

A few years later in the room below the Regent House, a brilliant, irritable, not very happy Dutchman began to teach a few of us a little Greek. He thought it was a failure. It was slow work, not much approved of by good people at the fish-stalls on Peas Hill. Also, he may have grudged the

labour wasted on such pupils—all except Bullock
—Bullock of Queens'. The residential system is
important. You can talk in a man's rooms. If
would-be benefactors of our Universities would
understand this, they could earn as lasting gratitude
as Fisher.

In Erasmus' rooms at Queens' Bullock might
find him reading Origen—*de Principiis* perhaps—
that passage about a God-implanted thirst for
knowledge of God's Truth and of the causes of
things, surely not implanted as a lure, doomed to
disappointment.[1] This is the true history of the
rebirth of Science; it wasn't due to rediscovery of
facts. Or else Erasmus might be writing a gay
essay—too gay, too petulant . . . brilliant, as they
used to say of Verrall and of Walter Headlam and
Jane Harrison and Cornford. . . . No bad sign
when that is said! But even more inspiring was it
if you found him poring over the Greek Testament
—the first Greek text that was ever to be printed.
It had mistakes, I am told, but it held the field for
three and a half centuries. Hort and Westcott
weren't the men to despise it. What is more
important, it gave our scholars a sound basis for
the making of the English Bible, the best gift of
the Renaissance to us all. Its principles were
scientific! Accuracy in establishing the facts, the
letter; reason and imagination in interpreting the
facts. I wonder—I speak as a fool, but I wonder
—what would Bacon's *Novum Organon* have been

[1] Quoted by Prof. H. G. Wood, *Christianity and Civilization*, p. 39.

if he had not been disciplined in the sound, generous tradition of Erasmus and his English friends?

Have we learnt all we had to learn? Can we at length dispense with the discipline of Latin? With the nourishment of Greek?

"Fie, how these mortals blame us gods!" said Zeus, "and say their troubles come from us! But they themselves by their own folly also, have griefs beyond their portion."[1]

Erasmus hated war and humbug, and in Europe, on the not very short run, he has failed. We need his spirit still. Luther disliked him and his principles, and so did most of Luther's enemies. More than all, they feared, as some still fear, the implications of his preference for the Greek fathers; his sane view of the ancient wisdom as a preparation for the Gospel, a preparation needed in all generations—God-given as the visions of the prophets were. It was this sane view of inspiration that seemed dangerous. Have we all, even now, listened to the appeal from the perfervid heat of the desert to the kinder thoughts of Alexandria, the clearer eyes of Athens, the charity of Tarsus at its best, the decent Jewish goodness of St. James, which Luther scorned, and to the loving understanding heart of John—all of which, I dare to say, Erasmus knew well in his own heart was a prayer, and an appeal to Him who also failed, as the world reckons failure.

[1] *Od.* i, 32 ff.

21

If Luther and his enemies had understood even a little, how much cruelty and wicked folly might not Germany and Europe have been spared.

Are you asking what has this to do with poetry? This isn't relevant? Isn't it? Most earnestly, though with some diffidence, I say it is.

> This spiritual love cannot exist
> Without imagination.

You remember the encounter with Egmondan? [1]

Erasmus. Let us proceed to argument. Imagine that I. . . .

Egmondan. I don't imagine. I won't imagine. That is your business. You poets imagine, and you always tell lies.

There we have it. As Pindar says, "Those whom Zeus hath not made his friends are filled with consternation when they hear the Muses." [2]

We English have been fortunate. Throughout our history there runs a golden thread of common sense and humour. What's the secret? Strange as it may seem, imagination fed by Poetry. The poetry first of the home, the child in the cradle, the mother, the old people by the fire; the poetry of the fields, the sky, the sea. But also the poetry of humanism: and, in those great days, of Christian and of scientific humanism too.

Think of More, planning Utopia and preaching

[1] Allen, iv, p. 384, quoted by Dr. Elliott Binns in his *Hulsean Lectures*, p. 73.
[2] Pindar, *Pythians*, i, 23.

toleration—even a pagan, he thought, could do better than we Christians, shame upon us!— giving his daughter Greek because a woman ought to have as good gifts as a man (Margaret justified him); writing to his good wife, "I beseech you, with your household and my children to be merry in the Lord."

Think of Colet, with no Greek himself, determined that the boys of Paul's should not be cheated of it.

Think of Cheke, and Ascham and a host of little domini and parsons, who taught Oxford, Cambridge, and King Edward and Sir William Cecil and the rich boys and the poor boys in the village schools and parsonages all over the country, each contributing his share to that first efflorescence of the English character and genius which we call the age of Shakespeare and of Marlowe.

Think of Ben Jonson, and by all means think of Milton. What a delight, what an experience for any boy who naturally takes to Milton, to learn Greek, Italian, and Latin. . . . Start that sort of boy with Milton and then try. Don't ask him the meaning of the words, or the grammar of the sentences. Just tell him what they are, if you think it will help. And teach him how to use a crib.

Better even than that is the thought of Whichcote, the kind puritan from Emmanuel. He didn't make quite such a stir in the philosophical world as certain other Platonists of the day. But he wouldn't take the Provostship of King's until he was allowed to pay a pension out of his own stipend to the loyalist who was evicted—for he said: "I will not leave the certain law of charity for an uncertain doctrine." "We are all fallible," he said. "We should suppose we may be mistaken. But the spirit of man is the candle of the Lord. To go against reason is to go against God. *Quotidie depono aliquem errorem.*"

We don't owe everything to St. Augustine, marching his monks from Dover, singing, with the silver cross before; nor to Theodore of Tarsus, founding our first Greek Grammar School; nor to York and Jarrow; nor even to Erasmus, More and Colet. But we still need Greek, especially Greek poetry from Homer to the Gospels. Even a very little Greek helps much. It isn't a mere accident the Gospels are in Greek. They can't be honestly interpreted except through the same light that came into the world by the Spirit, speaking to the writers. In Greek? In Aramaic? To each according to the measure of his love and understanding. Greek poetry is the poetry of freedom, friendship, reason: and the Gospel, as interpreted by simple hearts, is the poetry of kindness, good will, not to men of good will only—faithful unto death.

Happy days, you say, when men had leisure for such studies and for daydreams. We are busy, planning a more healthy world. Let me remind you of a certain Dr. William Harvey, a Folkestone lad, a yeoman's son, who was for some five years at King's School, Canterbury, learning Greek and Latin, then came up to Caius in 1593, and for three years read "*Classics, Dialectic, Physics.*" That was the normal balanced education of most Cambridge men till mid-Victorian days.

Harvey went next to Padua, studied medicine under Fabricius, came home to London, built up a good practice, and in 1628, when he was fifty, published a little book about the circulation of the blood. His practice mightily fell off. It was believed by the vulgar he was crack-brained. All the physicians were against him. But he did contribute something to the health of a new order.

What's the moral? Not that Harvey owed his genius to the classics. Alexander the Great did not owe his genius to his tutor, Aristotle, or to Homer. But my friend and teacher, Dr. Glover, used to tell me that we owe a debt to Homer for so educating Alexander that his genius was a blessing, not a curse, to the whole world.

As for Harvey, we must give some credit to his mother, "a comfortable, friendly matron," as her epitaph records. She was in his thoughts, I think, when he composed his dedication to King Charles: "The heart of animals is the foundation of their life, the sun of their microcosm, that upon which all growth depends."

And I am sure he thought of Caius and of his classics gratefully when, in that modest Introduction to his thesis, he quoted Demea's speech from Terence to explain what scientific method really

is: "However rationally one has calculated for
one's life, time, circumstance, experience, bring
always something new, and teach us something.
You find you don't know what you thought you
knew, and what you thought of first importance,
on experience, *experiundo*, you reject. That's what
has happened to me." [1]

Reluctantly we leave him, sitting under a hedge
at the battle of Edgehill with the Princes Charles
and James, reading a book about the generation of
eggs, till "a bullet from a great gun" made the
place unsuitable for further study of what he called
—and he had every right to call—"this branch of
the Republic of Letters."

Specialization, I believe, began to rear its ugly
head—in classics as in other fields of study—in
the eighteenth century, when Greek began to be
regarded as "like lace," a luxury for gentlemen.
Mr. Pope recalled the Muses with his *Iliad*. "A
very pretty poem," Bentley said, as if he knew as
much as Pope or Parson Adams about that! "A
very pretty poem, but we must not call it Homer."
As if we ever did! Pope tried to tell us something
of what Homer heard from life and from the
Muses, and had sung for him. He did it "pretty
well." It wasn't, of course, what Homer says to us,
or said to Keats and Chapman. We must still go
back to Greek.

[1] Terence, *Adelphi*, 855 ff. Harvey's treatise was edited with a
charming biographical essay by Dr. Alex. Bowie, 1889.

But the poets have done their best, and Arnold and the Public Schools have done well too. What about poorer children? Greek was "lace," a luxury. We didn't give it them, though Hughes and Maurice and Lowes Dickinson have tried to keep the spark alive. Surely the time has come when boys and girls from every sort of home should have the best that we can give them.

In my undergraduate days an Oxford humanist, behind the voices of Euripides and Aristophanes, heard the Muses singing of the Bacchants and the Frogs. He sang for us, and we knew—not exactly what the Muses or Euripides had sung to him, but we did know they had sung to Murray something beautiful. Then a Cambridge humanist heard the same song, but it sounded different; he told us: and we knew that Verrall had heard something most exciting. And each one of us who read Euripides and Aristophanes after that found that to us they were saying something different again . . . and yet . . . to all of us they said—was it truth or like the truth?—that life's a mystery, full of cruelty and folly, not quite all of our own making, but what matters is the brave heart, and the mind that seeks the truth . . . and above all the love of friends.

What of Laughter? says the devil's advocate. What of Laughter? When James Fitzjames Stephen lay in his cradle in 1830, seventeen months old, great-uncle William Wilberforce, the glory of the Clapham sect, who did as much as

27

anyone to free some of the world's slaves, came to do homage to the future Judge of the High Court. He stood over the cradle. Round blue eyes, eyes of a Stephen, kind, but clear, and capable of wrath, opened, and the child said one word: "Funny!" he said, and his mother, a Venn, felt sure he would be clever.

"Funny!" he said. O Rabelais! O Aristophanes! O Byron! What terrible harm you will do if the children listen to you singing.

Aristophanes loved Athens, and the Symposium proves that Plato knew he had loved Socrates in spite of all. He didn't mean to hurt, and it hurt him terribly when Athens fell, and Socrates died for his vision, not of knowledge, but of something perhaps like it. Aristophanes never wrote a good play after that.

But before it happened, he composed the *Frogs*, when Athens was about to make her last, heroic effort. He wrote it first of all to say: "I was against the war, but now it is our life, and all we care for. Alcibiades has not done well. But let him help. Let us forgive each other and all try again." Secondly, he wrote it as a tribute to the poetry of Athens. It isn't an attack. He had thought, and he still thought, that the Sophists, with their good, bad or indifferent intellectual cookery, a brainstrust with good brains, but not much knowledge, nor much vision, *were* a danger; he had thought, and he still thought, that all the charm of Euripides, his psychological analysis of passions, his appeal to

28

logic against old tradition, and also the amazing
dialectic of a Socrates, were dangerous to things of
deepest value. On the short run I believe he was
partly right: not on the long run. For Socrates and
Plato the new dialectic meant a near approach to a
new vision which has helped us all. And yet—
when he pursued the road, long after Socrates was
dead, Plato himself began to trust too much to
abstract mathematical conceptions. He fell under
the spell of the idea, divorced from life. Descartes
was in a stuffy room when he discovered that the
only thing he could be certain of was thinking. I
wish Plato hadn't put "Let no one enter here who
has no mathematics" at the door of his academy.
I wish he had said "Let no one go away without
some Poetry, some Dialectics, and some Physics."
Better still, *Hinc lucem et pocula sacra* . . . though
it isn't the motto makes the University. It's the
men and women.

Now Euripides was dead and Athens in dire
peril. Aristophanes sent Dionysus as a young
enthusiast for modern fashions, with Xanthias, a
good, earthy, ordinary slave—who liked his master
and could laugh with him and at him—to fetch the
poet back. There's no bitterness, no heartlessness
in that. He sends them on their journey to the
shades, where the poetical youth is frightened and
the ordinary man is not, by bogeys, but the poet-
god can travel in the grim old ferryman's boat,
not Xanthias: even so, the poet has to work his
passage: and he hears the songs the poor old

29

lonely ferryman thinks beautiful—the frog-songs
—which I fear the god thinks "muck"—not
Charon. To some of us that's touching.

After this introduction, a supreme example of
this poet's power of blending (as life blends) the
farcical and the sublime, the young god finds himself confronted with a question which he hasn't
faced before—at any rate, not lately. What do you
really feel about poetry?

It is exquisitely done, and rarely understood—
though it was loved by crowded audiences, boys
and girls, in 1936.

The contest of Euripides and Aeschylus opens
with prayer to the Muses. Then the poet of
Eleusis prays:

> Demeter, by whose bread my mind was nurtured,
> May I be worthy of thy mysteries.

That is Aeschylus. Then, for Euripides, this delightful blend of earnestness and fun and courtesy.

Euripides would rather be excused. "No, thank
you. I have divinities of my own." "By all means
pray to your new gods."

A model of the courtesy of Athens at her best.

> Aether whereon I pasture, eloquence
> And understanding and the critical nose!
> In all my argument, be my proofs made good.

This is serious as well as gay. The nearest approach
we find in Euripides to a positive religious doctrine,
is in fact his hint at a belief in an immortal, all-
embracing aether. Not unlike some modern
science.

But his prayer, "In any logos that I handle may I prove my case aright," is not to be despised.

Here, indeed, is the fundamental issue of all education. Is it not fundamental for the education which is life itself? May we reason rightly; may our souls be fed. Are the two prayers incompatible?

In the debate we have our fun, and so do the poets and their judge; but all the time the music of the mysteries persists.

We hear it as an undercurrent, and it moves us every time we hear the words, "exile, death, exile, sleep, life, argument, persuasion, poetry, life, and death."

At the end Dionysus votes for the more weighty of the two imponderables. He chooses Aeschylus, the poet of the mystery of life and death, but he still likes Euripides. One is so pleasant, but the other wise. Wise? Aeschylus wise? That is what Dionysus used to call Euripides. Now he has grown up.

"I come here for a poet." "Why a poet?"
"That Athens, saved, might keep her worship still." [1]

So the man who sang of Salamis and of Prometheus, of Athena's vote for mercy, and of Zeus "whoe'er He be," the Justicer, the Saviour, is chosen and brought back to life.

I don't think the world's adrift. Athens fell, and we say "Socrates died," yet Athens lives. The music of the *Oresteia*, with which the *Frogs* ends,

[1] *Frogs*, 1418 f. her sacred dances, χορούς.

31

noblest symbol of the effort Athens made to reconcile clear thinking with the gods of her tradition,
is not yet quite silent or forgotten.

> 'Twas Zeus who bade men tread
> The sober road of thought.
> 'Twas he whose ordinance decreed
> Ye needs must suffer, to be taught.
> Stern Grace, I ween, by Spirits given,
> By Spirits seated at the helm of heaven.[1]

I don't think the world's adrift. Stern Grace
still helps as well as hurts. And I am sure—the
clear eyes and kind voices of the gallant men and
women that I meet assure me—the good ship's
crew is fighting hard to keep on the right course.
It is our privilege to help, and to be helped.

[1] *Agam.* 174 ff.

HELICON

THE MUSES AND THEIR PUPIL

THE Muses understand us all and sympathize with most of us; and that is why, eight hundred years before the birth of Christ, they came one night to Hesiod in old Boeotia and taught him a new song.

He was a farmer and a farmer's son. When he was a boy, tradition says, his family had lived at Cume on the far side of the Aegean, on the coasts that had not suffered greatly in the dark days of the Dorian invasions. In Cume there was life. Homer's matchless voice had been heard there, and was loved. But Boeotia, dull Boeotia? Why on earth did father settle there, and buy a farm at Askra, of all places, "bad in winter, stuffy in the summer, never any good"? [1]

Father lived and died there, and his sons inherited. One, Perses, was a type we know, hard-faced, but not hard-working—clever. He contrived to get more than his fair share of the farm. He bribed the squires and won his case. The other, Hesiod, was also of a type East Anglians and Yorkshiremen know well, hard-headed, horny-handed, honest, discontented, well aware that the good earth gives nought for nought. If

[1] *Works and Days*, 640.

you slack or cheat, it's at your peril. A hard world,
but there's rough justice somehow, sometimes.

Happily he had a sense of humour, grim but
healthy, and, thanks perhaps to father, he knew
Homer. He himself had stirrings, dreams, and
tried his hand at verses—practical stuff as a rule,
none of your high romance for Askra; good advice
about crops, beasts and seasons; moral essays,
pointed at his brother and the squires; sound
ethics and sound economics and no nonsense.

Then, as he kept his sheep one night on Helicon,
he saw, or dreamt he saw, the Muses. After he had
looked and listened and been taught by them, he
sang, like our own Caedmon after he had met the
angel, a far better song than he or anybody ever
dreamt that he could sing.[1]

Muses of Helicon, so begin the song,
To whom the high and holy heights of Helicon belong,
Delicately dancing round the deep blue spring
And all about the altar of the Heavenly King,
Bathing in the river-springs to make their bodies fine,
Permeios and Olmeios and Hippocrene divine,
Then upward to the highest height of Helicon they throng
To the dance of love and beauty, and their feet are swift and
     strong.

Thence it was they came to me, veiled in robes of night,
Moving through the shadows, and their voices of delight
Sang of Zeus, the Lord and King, and of His Consort told,
Hera, Queen of Argos, whose sandals are of gold,
And Athena, the King's daughter, whose eyes are wondrous grey,
Artemis, the Huntress, and Apollo, Lord of Day,
And Poseidon, the World-Holder, who can shake the world, men
     say;

---

[1] *Theogony*, 1–29.

Themis, who is modest, Aphrodite, who is bold,
Dione fair and Phoebe, with her coronet of gold,
The Morning and the Sun-God and Selene, shining bright,
Leto and Iapetos and Cronos' crafty spite,
And Earth and the vast Ocean and Night in sable stole,
And all the other holy gods who know not death nor dole.

These were they who came to me, the singer of the song,
Hesiod, who kept my sheep high Helicon along;
And this was what they said to me, these daughters of the King,
The Muses, the Olympians, who taught me how to sing—
  Shame on you, shepherds, greedy-guts, uncouth!
We know the way to tell a tale and make it like the truth,
And, when we please, we also know the way to speak plain sooth.

Streng wissenschaftlich, learned friends assure us
that these lines mean simply (*a*) that Homer didn't
tell the truth, though he professed to, and (*b*) that
the Boeotian economico-didactic school could be
relied on for the facts. Nonsense! The Muses
meant: "If you hear voices in the fields or at the
forge—though there's too much chattering there
—or on the hills, they may be ours. They may be.
We are friends, the daughters of the King. Don't
stop your ears or run away, for what you hear *may*
be the truth, or something like it. Zeus only
knows the truth, but we know more than you, for
we were taught by one who knows much more
than we, Apollo. Listen, then, and sing yourself.
But keep your head. Remember. When these
fancies come they may not all be true. It is for you
to judge. Some voices come from us and some
from far worse singers. *You* are the judge. It's
your own education that we have at heart, as well
as other people's."

So they cut a laurel-bough and gave it him, and breathed on him and put a voice in him and bade him sing of all that is and all that shall be.[1]

They bade me sing of the birth of the gods, and to sing of themselves they bade,
With the Muses first, and the Muses last, and the gods who are
always glad.
But enough of me, and the rock and the tree, and the tale of a
shepherd-lad.

Sing we of the Muses and the song the Muses sing
To the Father in Olympus for the pleasure of the King,
Weaving all that has been or is or yet shall be
In a garland of sweet singing, in a flood of melody.
Oh, pleasant is that music. It blossoms like a spray
Of lilies, and the palace of the Thunder-Lord grows gay
Till the Halls of Heaven and the snow-clad peaks of white
Olympus ring
With echoes of the deathless voice of the Muses, when they sing
What was in the beginning, the awful primal birth
Of the sanctities begotten by Heaven of Mother Earth,
And the gods who came thereafter and who saved the world
from dearth.

Peal after peal, with repetition, varying and heightening what soon become familiar themes made new, the music takes us to Olympus, where these goddesses, conceived by Memory in the embrace of Zeus the Counsellor, were born, a little way below the highest height, and have their dwelling and their dancing-places still,

With the Graces for their neighbours, close to the place where
Love
Lodges in time of festival . . .[2]

The shaping and reshaping of the gods in

[1] *Theogony*, 34–46.   [2] 60–64.

beauty was perhaps the greatest service Hesiod and Homer did for Greece and for ourselves. Such gods and goddesses as these are human, sometimes all too human; but they are incomparably better than the crude imaginations of the heathen. The thought, the loving worship of them, educated Greece and, in the long run, taught her cleverest, and some of her best citizens, to look for something nobler still. Had it not been for that, Xenophanes, the sophist, Heraclitus, the eccentric egoistic genius, could not possibly have reached the heights from which they railed on Homer for imperfect notions of divinity. Not even Plato, had he not been educated by the poets, could have won the transcendental vision for the sake of which, with reverent impertinence he banished Homer from his own ideal Republic.

At last we reach the Presence, and before the Majesty of Zeus enthroned the Muses sing again; and as we listen to the lovely names of all the "Nine, Divine," we have forgotten Askra and the hardships of the farm, the scoundrel Perses, the corrupt, oppressive magistrates, the idlers who prefer to gossip at the forge. Is this escapist stuff? Not quite, for we are told before the end how, if Calliope and her fair sisters

> look upon the birth
> Of any Prince Zeus-nurtured and have set him high in place,
> Upon his lips they do infuse a dew of special grace,
> And sweet as honey are his words. The people of the land
> Look to their prince in reverence for judgment and command
> Because he judgeth righteously, with wisdom, to abate

The heat of high contention when it grows inordinate;
For a Prince doth most show wisdom when a folk infatuate
Is turned in the assembly from folly and from wrong
Right easily and gently by the suasion of his tongue.[1]

That thought, as reinterpreted by later generations, gave us the Aeschylean doctrine of Divine
Persuasion which converts even the Furies to Kind
Goddesses. It gave us also the conception of a
social order governed by consent, not violence.

As for the poet himself, and for ourselves, his
humbler neighbours, the Muses offer this:

Thrice happy is the man the Muses love;
They make his lips with joyfulness and melody to move.
And he to whom strange trouble comes, distracted and distressed,
Sick at heart with sorrowing, woefully oppressed,
If a servant of the Muses, a poet, makes a song
Of the heroes or the blessed gods to whom the Heavens belong,
He soon forgets his heaviness, nor thinks of grief again,
For the good gifts of the Muses have turned away his pain.[2]

That is how the Muses teach their pupils still.
First they rebuke our gross absorption in the
economic problem. Then they show us something
of the wonder and the "hidden beauty" of the
world. Is the revelation true? Not wholly, and not
always. Zeus knows all. The Muses bid us listen,
wonder, and reflect and judge. It is just that
liberty of choice that most attracts us. Thought is
free, and leads to strange conclusions. The best
poets often contradict themselves.

For Hesiod, on the day he met the Muses, the
result was that he told how from primeval Chaos

[1] 81–90.   [2] 96–104.

38

the broad-bosomed Earth emerged and Love, the fairest of immortals; how from Chaos came black Night and the deep murk of Erebos: then, out of Night, the clear bright Air and Day. Fantastic births ensued, misrule and misbegotten monsters, powers of hate and craft and cruelty at war, till after grievous travail, with much bitterness and suffering, the race of the Olympians emerged and order triumphed.

On the whole, in the result, it is a happy story. But what of mortals? Have they much improved? At Askra Hesiod saw no reason to believe it. There were times when he exclaimed, "I wish I had been born in the good days or had not lived till better days return." He dreamt, as we all dream, of an imagined Golden Age, perhaps far in the past, perhaps far in the future, certainly not here and now.[1]

The gods who rule Olympus, while Cronos held his place
As King of gods, created here on earth a Golden Race.

   A race of mortal men were they, but like the gods they lived
     their day
Free from trouble, full of joy, and growing old without annoy,
With hand and foot still strong;
A life of bright and pure delight, exempt from care and wrong,
And when they died, they seemed to fall asleep.

Wishful thinking? Yes, but wishful thinking often helps. Part of the dream we still believe, in spite of all, may yet come true, or anyhow prove much more "like the truth" than the confusion and

[1] *Works and Days*, 109–126.

distress of our own time:

> The earth was theirs, and theirs the yield,
> Unlaboured of the willing field,
> And all were free, and all might have
> The good land and the gifts it gave
> In safe tranquillity to keep.
> And so they dwelt among their sheep,
> Passing rich and richly blest;
> And when at last they went to rest
> In earth, the Counsellor on high
> Decreed they should not wholly die,
> But as good watchman spirits go
> Up and down and to and fro,
> Wrapp'd in mist from mortal sight,
> Watching all the wrong and right
> Done upon the earth, and so,
> Princes once among the living,
> Princely gifts they still are giving.

John Keats, I fancy, thought of that when, on the blank page of the *Fair Maid of Perth*, he wrote:

> Bards of Passion and of Mirth,
> Ye have left your souls on earth . . .

In their books, he meant, which we can read. But this says something more—

> Have ye souls in heaven too,
> Double-lived in regions new?
> Yes . . . ye live on high and then
> On the earth ye live again;
> And the souls ye left behind you
> Teach us here the way to find you.

Wishful thinking? Yes, but wishful thinking also helps. Not that the Golden Age is the end of Hesiod's story or of ours. It is followed by an Age of Silver, when young people spend a hundred years as mother's darlings, frolicsome and silly, and then suddenly grow up. They only live a short time longer, miserable, foolish, doing one another bad turns and neglecting good old customs and religion. Zeus, one hardly needs to say, is much offended, and earth covers them. Even so we, of a later generation, call them "blessed" second only to the Golden Race, and still respect them.

How charitable that is, how Greek. With what a smile the poet must have said it. He habitually grumbled, and especially at other people's faults, but he understood spoilt children and it seems, he sympathized a little with them.

The Race of Bronze was worse. With their bronze tools and brazen houses—they themselves were made of wood, the toughest wood, the sort from which men make their spear-shafts—they quarrelled and destroyed each other and went down to Hades unrenowned, unsung.

After these—surprisingly as commentators tell us—Zeus created a new, juster race. Heroes and demi-gods we call them. These also fell in war, raiding for cattle in the fortress area of Thebes or fighting overseas for Helen. But when they died, Zeus sent them to the Islands of the Blest by the deep pools of Ocean. There they live, heart-free, and thrice a year earth gives them her good harvest, honey-sweet. And Cronos is their governor.

A break in the historical and factual sequence? So the learned say. But the poetic scheme and our own hearts demand this exquisite return to Cronos and to happiness, which is a tribute to the work of Homer's Muse, before we plunge into our present anxious, gloomy world.

What of the men of the fifth Race? Would it were not my fate
To be one of them. Would I had died, or had been born too late.
These are the race of the men of iron. Ah, never shall they
Have respite from tears and trouble by night or day.
They dwindle to ruin, alas : for the gods shall lay
Care after anxious care on them. Yet, though the worst befall,
Good will be mixed with the evil in spite of all.[1]

This, his own race, Hesiod declares, will perish, when the children are born with grey hairs. Then Chaos will return, not the Chaos of the elements, the primal powers at war, but moral chaos among men.

Hesiod's description of that fearful time reminds us of Thucydides' account of the effects of civil war in Greece, as well as many things that we have seen in our own time. Fathers will be estranged from children, children from their fathers. Might will be right. One man will sack another's city. None will respect the man who keeps his oath and promise. Men will praise the evil-doer for his violence. Reverence will be no more, and foul-mouthed Envy will walk scowling among wretched mortals, till Modesty and Righteous Indignation, veiling their fair bodies in white robes, will pass from wide-wayed earth to live with the immortal gods in heaven, leaving with us mortals bitter sorrow and no help at all.

Perhaps we understand a little better than we could ten years ago how Hesiod felt about the

[1] *Works and Days,* 174–179.

42

heroes and the iron age and what might follow. It is some consolation to remember that he wrote not very long before the dawn of a much better age, the age of the Ionian renaissance and the prime of Athens.

THE NOD OF ZEUS

Sing, Goddess, of the Wrath of Achilles, son of Peleus,
Fatal and accursèd Wrath, for on the Greeks it laid
Innumerable Griefs, and many souls of stalwart heroes
Hurled headlong to the house of Death, and of their bodies made
A prey for dogs, a feast for birds, fulfilling the Design
Of Zeus. Begin the story when the King, the son of Atreus,
First fell apart in quarrel from Achilles, the divine.

DID Homer really think the Muse inspired him?
Did he suppose she really helped him as he sifted
and resifted the crude matter of the saga, pondering, reshaping, reinterpreting old, often barbarous,
tradition, and exploiting for fresh purposes a rich
inheritance of diction, rhythm, pattern, themes and
images? I think he did. He asked her help, and
by that very thought was helped. Not that the
Muse does everything for him or anyone. Some
things he had to think of for himself; others "the
goddess" put into his heart. So, as he told his tale,
he was vouchsafed a clearer, kinder vision of life's
paradox, its beauty and its baffling cruelty; the
courage that can turn endurance to a triumph, and
the frailty that can cause a hero, like a petulant
child, to break and throw away what in his heart
he values more than life itself. But even so, in
spite of man's perversity and the caprice of an
unruly family of gods, he saw, or seemed to see,
however dimly apprehended, the promise of a

pattern and a purpose more august: "Sing, Goddess, of the Wrath, and of the Grief and Death it
caused, in the fulfilment of the plan of Zeus."

Which of the gods first brought these men together in contention?
The son of Zeus and Leto. He was angry with the King
For the insult he had put upon his priest, the man of Chrysa,
And the folk were perishing:
He had come to the swift ships with precious gifts for ransoming
His daughter, and he bore the golden sceptre in his hands,
Wreath'd about with sacred bands, of Apollo, the Far-Shooter;
And he prayed to the Achaeans, making supplication most
To the twain, the sons of Atreus, the rulers of the host:
 Sons of Atreus and the rest of you, ye strongly-greaved Achaeans
May the gods who hold Olympus grant the boon for which you
  pray,
That you sack the town of Priam and return safe home again;
But release to me my daughter. Precious ransom I will pay.
Nay, accept it and release her, for the reverence that ye owe
To the son of Zeus, Apollo, the Wielder of the Bow.
Then the rest of them were fain
To do reverence to the priest and take the ransom he would
  pay,
But it did not please the heart of Agamemnon, son of Atreus,
With a word of harsh authority he sent him shamed away.
 Do not let me find you, greybeard, by the hollow galleys lingering,
Or coming here again, for this I promise, if you come,
Little the wreath'd sceptre of your archer-god shall profit you.
I shall not loose your daughter. In our Argos, far from home,
She shall weave the web and wait upon my bed before I do,
And so grow old. Provoke me not. For your own safety, go.
He spoke, and that old man grew very fearful and obeyed.
Silently, in grief, he went his way. Along the shore
Of the sounding sea he stepped; and he stood apart and prayed
Many prayers to King Apollo whom the bright-tressed Leto
 bore.
 Prince of the silver Bow, strong ward of Tenedos, incline
To hear me, Lord of Cilla, God of Chrysa. If the shrine,
Mouse-god, that I roof'd for thee, find favour in thine eyes,
Or if ever I have pleased thee with the smoke of sacrifice,
Fat thighs of goats and oxen, grant the boon for which I pray,

That for these my tears these Danaans beneath thy shafts may pay.
He spoke, and he was heard. Apollo harkened to his word,
Striding down Olympus' peaks with anger in his heart.
On his shoulder was the Bow, and the covered quiver, fraught
With the arrows of the god: they rattled on his shoulder in his
  anger, as he strode
Ever onward, like the Night.
And he sat him down apart from the ships and aimed a dart,
Ranging among the mules at first, and the swift dogs; but then
He shot a sharp shaft at the men, and shot and shot again.
The pyres on which they burnt their dead were many and were
  bright.

It is not surprising that the poets, not the
scholars, have best understood this prelude,[1] its
pattern and its function in the poem. After all, it
is the poet's business, as we have been told by one
who is himself an admirable poet, Mr. Day Lewis,
in his talks on *The Poetic Image*,[2] to seek pattern,
and to recognize it when he sees it, and then "to
build his perceptions into a poetic form which by
its urgency and coherence will persuade us of
their truth."

Mr. Day Lewis may not have been thinking
specially of Homer's pattern-making, pattern-
seeking, when he wrote those words, but they
reminded me of Homer. So did his next sentence:

He (the poet) is in the world, we may say, to bear witness
to the principle of love, since love is as good a word as any for
that human reaching-out of hands towards the warmth in all
things which is the source and passion of his song. Love is this
to him first: but it is more; he apprehends it as a kind of necessity
by which all things are bound together, and in which, could

---

[1] *Iliad*, i, 1–52.
[2] *Clark Lectures*, 1946 (Jonathan Cape), p. 36 f.

the whole pattern be seen, their contradictions would appear reconciled.

On those last five words I pause. All contradictions? Has the poet any such assurance? We see through a glass darkly, and for most of us it is enough to say that both the poet and the man of science seek some sort of pattern, each in his own field of observation, and that both work on because of an essentially poetic intuition (or assumption) that the more we understand of anything, the more it will appear to make some sort of sense.

Be that as it may, and by whatever processes of thought, experience and meditation Homer's vision came to him, his version of the tragedy of Troy is not a tale of sound and fury, signifying nothing. The "source and passion of his song" is certainly "a reaching-out of hands towards the warmth in all things," a deep human sympathy. In that respect he is the one Greek poet we can truly call Shakespearean. Sophocles, in his latest phase, and, on occasion, Aristophanes come nearest. As for the pattern both of narrative and images, if recognized and understood, as it so rarely is by critics and dissectors, it can prove a master-key to our appreciation and enjoyment of the poet's work. So far from being merely ornamental, it is Homer's means of giving both "coherence" to his story and persuasive "urgency" to his discovery (or intuition or assumption), a discovery far more important than mere verbal pattern-making, of a moral order in the world, an order on the whole

47

beneficent, for which his symbol was "the plan of Zeus."

Of our English poets none has understood this better than our own great pattern-maker, Milton. That is why he thought of Homer when he prayed the "Heavenly Muse" to sing

> Of Man's first Disobedience and the Fruit
> Of that forbidden Tree whose mortal taste
> Brought Death into the world and all our Woe
> With loss of Eden, till one Greater Man
> Restore us . . . ;

and again, when, soaring "high above the Aonian Mount" (where Hesiod met the Muses), he invoked the Spirit who made Chaos pregnant to instruct him:

> What in me is high
> Illumine. What is low, raise and support,
> That to the height of this great argument
> I may assert eternal Providence
> And justify the ways of God to men.

Indeed the whole grand catalogue—"Man's Disobedience . . . Death and *all* our Woe . . . one greater Man . . . God . . . Spirit . . . God to men" —is not so much a challenge from the Christian to the pagan poet, as a sincere and, for John Milton, humble tribute to the truth and deep significance of Homer's intuition.

Nor is this all. The tragic theme of "Disobedience, Death and all our Woe," developed in the sequel to "Revolt, guilt, envy and revenge and

impious War," leads on to the tremendous climax
of the Wrath of the Omnipotent, hurling the rebel
angels down in flames, to lie

> Nine times the space that measures day and night . . .
> Confounded, though immortal.

And after that, after the high debate in the Infernal
Congregation, and the vision of the Adversary's
fatal enterprise, it is again with mention of the
Muses and of Homer that the poet, reinvoking
the Celestial Light—

> Shine inward, and the mind through all her powers
> Irradiate . . .,

enters the Court of Heaven, where the divine discourse, the rapture of the music and the adoration
of the Father and the Son, seem to give promise
of a resolution of the tragic discord.

So in the *Iliad* the central tragic theme, Wrath,
Grief and Death, is first restated and applied to
Agamemnon's sin against the suppliant, Apollo's
priest, and so leads up to the tremendous climax
of Apollo's vengeance and the plague. Nor is the
counter-theme, fulfilment of the plan of Zeus, forgotten in the sequel. It is heard, as we shall see,
with a new note of promise, at the height of the
dispute in the Assembly, when Athena's intervention saves Achilles from the worst dishonour: it is
heard again, in its full majesty and mystery, after
the wrong done to Achilles by the King, the
prayer to Thetis, the propitiation of Apollo, and
the appeal to Zeus of Thetis for her son, in the

high god's response, the Nod which shakes
Olympus, and the word—"These things shall be
my care."

Nine days through the army went the arrows of the god,
But on the tenth Achilles called the people to their place
Of Assembly. White-armed Hera, when she saw the people
      perishing,
Gave him the thought, because she sought
To do the Danaans grace.[1]

This intervention of the "white-armed goddess"
surely comforts us a little. It is the poet's way of
telling us Achilles acted on an impulse of just
indignation and of pity which we share. Rash as
the act of calling the Assembly is, our sympathies
are with him. His appeal to Agamemnon comes
from a generous, brave, anxious heart.

Son of Atreus, now indeed I think with purpose unaccomplish'd,
Baffled we shall go back home unless we all are dead,
If we Danaans must suffer war with pestilence as well.
Come, let us ask a prophet or a priest or an interpreter
Of dreams—for dreams are also sent by Zeus—that he may tell
What trespasses have brought on us the wrath of high Apollo,
What vow hath been forgotten, what oblation left unpaid,
That by savour of sweet sacrifice of lambs or goats unblemish'd
We may turn the god from anger and the pestilence be stayed.[2]

Agamemnon makes no move and gives no
answer. Calchas, the prophet, says:

Achilles, well-beloved of Zeus . . . [3]

It is an epithet not often used by Homer for a hero.
Its use here by the prophet is significant.

[1] *Il.* i, 53 ff.   [2] 59 ff.   [3] $\Delta \iota \dot{\iota}$ $\phi \acute{\iota} \lambda \varepsilon$, 73 ff.

Achilles, well-beloved of Zeus, you bid me to declare
The reason for the anger of Apollo, the Far-Shooter.
I will speak if you will listen and a solemn oath will swear
That readily by word and deed you mean to take my part;
For I think that I shall anger the great Lord of the Achaeans,
The Prince we all obey;
And a prince is very mighty who is angry with a commoner;
He may nurse his wrath in silence; he may cloak it for the day
But will cherish it thereafter, and the purpose of his heart
In the end he will fulfil.
Will you answer for my safety then? Look to it if you will.

Achilles' answer, though we like him for its courage, is a blunder. Such a challenge to a king at such a time breeds mischief.

Whatever be your knowledge, speak it bravely, for I swear,
By Apollo, well-beloved of Zeus, to whom your vows are paid ...
While I live upon this earth, while I see this light of day,
No man beside the hollow ships, not one, shall dare to lay
Strong hands upon you for your hurt—not one of them, I say,
No, not even Agamemnon, though he maketh it his boast
To be far the best, above the rest of the Achaean host.[1]

Calchas speaks. The plague is due to Agamemnon's sin, and till the captive girl is given to her father without ransom, without price, Apollo cannot be appeased.

He spoke, and down he sat ; and in their midst upstood
King Agamemnon, sorely vexed. His heart was black with stress
Of wrath, his eyes like shining fire, and thus he made address
To Calchas first among the rest, as boding him no good—
   Prophet of evil, never yet has any word of thine
Been good, because thy pleasure is things evil to divine ...
Even so, if it is better, I consent. She shall go free;
I would rather have the people saved than see them perishing.
But prepare another portion straight and render it to me

---

[1] 85 ff.

As my prize. It is not even seemly that the King
Should be portionless alone among the Argives, and my own
They are taking to be given to another, as you see.[1]

The demand is indefensible and the tone arrogant,
but Achilles still keeps self-control enough to say
the King shall have threefold, nay fourfold compensation when Troy falls. From Agamemnon
that elicits only a vague threat.

> You say, "Release the maid"—
Well and good, if the great-hearted Achaeans find for me
Another prize well-pleasing, to requite me worthily.
But, if they will not give it, I shall take from whom I please,
From Odysseus or from Ajax, his portion—or your own . . . [2]

At the mere hint Achilles instantly takes fire.
Agamemnon of all people, has no right to treat the
honour of his fellow-princes thus. He counters
threat with threat.[3]

O cloaked about with shamelessness, O greedy, guileful heart,
How can any Greek be glad to go a journey at your call?
Or to fight upon your part?
Did the Trojans bring me hither? Have I any grudge at all
Against the Trojan spearmen? Did the Trojans ever come
To carry off my cattle or my horses from my home,
Or to spoil my crops for me
In deep-loamed Phthia, nurse of men ? Beyond the sounding sea
Over many shadowy mountains, far away from Troy it lies.
No, shameless one, it was not they, but you who brought me here,
In a service done to you and to Menelaus too,
Dog-face, although you heed it not at all, but only say
That you mean to take away
What was given me as mine, and the winning cost me dear . . .
I shall go back home to Phthia! Better far to sail away,
Home in my beakéd galleys, home. I have no mind to stay,
Toiling to make you rich, and have no honour in your eyes.

---

[1] 101 ff.   [2] 135 ff.   [3] 149 ff.

With that the quarrel rises to its climax. Agamemnon answers:

Fly, if you are so inclined. I make no prayer to you
To stay on my account. There are others here to do
To the King all honour due,
And most of all the Counsellor, High Zeus; for in his care
Are the princes of the world, not one of whom, I swear,
Is hateful to my heart as you, for strife is your delight:
You are valiant in war, and still you quarrel and you fight,
But if valiant you are, it is a god who gives you might.
   Go, take your ships and men. Go, get you home, and reign
At home among your Myrmidons—what matter if you do?
I gave nothing for your anger. I myself can threaten too.
Even as Apollo takes from me the maid of Chrysa,
I will send her in a ship of mine, with men of mine, safe home;
And even so will take from you your fair-cheeked maid of Brisa,
Your prize of honour from your tent. Yes, I myself will come,
And take here there, to teach you I am better far than you,
That other men may know it, and another man may fear
To esteem himself my equal or to call himself my peer.[1]

Impetuous, headstrong, generous, Achilles came
to Troy because he was in love with fame. He
knew, or thought he knew, that he would die there,
but it seemed worth while, because he would have
honour in the sight of heaven and praise from all
men both in life and death. Now Agamemnon has,
in full Assembly, wantonly, outrageously insulted
him, made him seem nothing, less than nothing;
and the youth, in the first shock of anger, stands a
moment, wavering, his honour in the balance.[2]

He spoke, and Peleus' son was sorely wounded by the word,
And his heart within his shaggy breast divided, pondering,

---

         [1] i, 173 ff.   [2] i, 188–222.

Should he scatter the Assembly, should he draw the flashing
    sword,
And strike and kill the King,
Or check his anger in control?   But even while he strove,
Divided and perplex'd of soul, and even while he drew
The great sword from the scabbard, lo! Athena, from above,
By one who cherished both these men, in pity and in love
Was sent, by white-armed Hera, and invisible she flew
To all of them except to him: only Achilles knew.
She caught him by the bright hair back, and, turning in surprise
He look'd and saw 'twas Pallas, for the splendour of her eyes
Was fearful; and he cried *Art thou here again so soon?*
Child of the Aegis-bearer, art thou here, to look upon
The overweening pride of Agamemnon, Atreus' son?
I will tell thee of my purpose, and I think it shall be done:
For his arrogance outrageous he shall perish here anon.

    But the grey-eyed goddess answered, *Will you hearken to my*
      word?
I have come to check your passion.   I am sent you from above,
By the white-armed Hera sent to you, in pity and in love
For both you men.   Come leave your strife, and do not draw the
    sword.
Yet taunt him still with words you may, and bid him think upon
The future—for I promise you, and swear it shall be done,
For his arrogance this day he shall quit you and repay
Thrice as many precious gifts to you.   Now hear us and obey.

    The swift-footed Achilles made answer, and he said:
Ye have spoken.   Be it so.   It is better, for I know
That the gods must be obeyed.   Be it even as ye say;
For if mortal men obey the gods ye hear us when we pray.
He spoke, and on the silver hilt he check'd his heavy hand,
And back into the sheath again thrust home the mighty brand,
Neglecting not Athena's word; and she returned to Zeus, the
    Lord,
The Aegis-bearer, throned with all the gods in high Olympus'
    hall.

That is the first appearance of Athena in the long
tradition of Greek history and poetry.   She comes
to save a young man from disaster.   Had he killed

the King it would have meant the end of honour for him. He is saved from that.

The dispute goes on, and yet I think the tone, after Athena's intervention, subtly changes. Even Achilles, though his taunts are bitter—

Eyes of a dog, heart of a hind, sot, robber-prince . . . ,

is conscious of the transience of mortality. When he swears by the Sceptre which was once a living branch, we hear for the first time a theme from which, throughout the sequel, Homer is to make some of his noblest music:

I swear it by the Sceptre, which will never bud anew,
For the axe has done its work upon the mountain where it grew,
So stripping off both leaf and bark that never anything,
Nor twig nor leaf, may grow again, but only this bare trunk
    remain,
The staff our Judges take in hand
By ancient custom of the land and grace of Zeus, the King—
An oath that you will understand—I swear it, time shall bring
A longing for Achilles to the sons of the Achaeans,
Yea, to all of them alike, I swear. But nothing any more
Shall profit or avail you then, although your grief be sore,
And your angry heart be rent with affliction, and repent,
When many men shall fall to murderous Hector in the fight,
That the best of the Achaeans had no honour in your sight.[1]

That is the first mention in the *Iliad* of Hector. Nestor's talk of ancient chivalry has something of the same effect. He himself, as a survivor of three generations, is a symbol of mortality. The music of the close requires no comment.

[1] i, 225 and 234–244.

So they rose up from their places, still disputing stubbornly,
And they broke up their assembly at the galleys by the sea,
And the son of Peleus went to his ships and to his tent
With his friends, of whom the son of Menoetius was one.[1]

That is the first mention of Patroclus in the poem.

Presently Agamemnon sent his heralds to
Achilles' tent to fetch Briseis.[2]

Unwillingly they went beside the sea unharvested
Till they came to the encampment and the galleys of the
    Myrmidons:
And there beside his own black ship close to his tent he sat.
They saw him and he saw them too, but had no joy thereat.

Yet he received them with grave courtesy.

They stood before him full of fear: they reverenced the King,
And found no voice within their breast for speech or questioning.
In his own heart he read their thought and spoke to them this
    word:
  Give you good greeting, messengers of Zeus and mortals too.
Come closer, heralds, closer. I have no reproach for you,
But only for your Lord, who has sent you for the maid
Briseis. Then he said:
  Zeus-born Patroclus, bring her here and give her to these twain;
Yes, give her back again.
These two shall be my witnesses in sight of gods and men,
And in sight of that untoward prince, that mine is not the blame
When they need me most, to save the host from ruin and from shame.
He is now distracted quite, and he cannot judge aright
Of the past and of the future, nor take counsel any more
For the safety of his people in the peril of the war.
  He had spoken, and Patroclus, when he heard his friend's
    command,
Brought fair Briseis from the tent and gave her to the men,
And they made their way again to the ships of the Achaeans,
And the woman went with them unwillingly. And then
Achilles wept.

---

[1] i, 305–307.   [2] i, 326–363.

She went "unwillingly." That tells us much.

Achilles wept. He left his friends, and, seated on the strand
Of the grey sea, gazing on the wine-dark waters, made
Many prayers to his dear mother. Thus, with lifted hands, he
    prayed:
  Mother, Zeus the Thunderer, because I am thy son,
Should have given me much honour, for I have not long to live.
Yet no honour doth He give,
For the lordly son of Atreus, Agamemnon, utterly
Hath shamed me, taking back my prize to keep it for his own.
  So he spoke, and wept, and his dear mother heard the cry.
Sitting with her father in the deep pools of the sea,
She heard, and swiftly, like a mist, from the grey waters came.
She sat beside him on the strand. She called him by his name,
And touched him gently with her hand, still weeping bitterly.
  My child, why are you weeping sore? What grief has moved you
    so?
Speak. Do not hide it in your heart, that both of us may know.

How wonderfully Homer understands. The
story, as the young man tells it to his mother, is less
than just to the Achaeans, and, as passion grows on
him, he ends with a petition so outrageous that it
puts him for the first time in the wrong.

  Go, sit by Zeus and pray to him and tell my tale for me.
Peradventure He will yield to you and give the Trojans victory,
Cooping the Achaeans at the ships and by the sea,
To be slaughtered shamefully,
Till they all shall know the blessedness of serving such an one,
And the folly he hath done,
And the lordly Agamemnon rue to-day and pay its price
When the best of the Achaeans had no honour in his eyes.[1]

He has been grossly, wantonly humiliated. We
can understand why he refuses for himself and for

_____
[1] i, 407–412.

57

his friend all further service in a questionable cause. According to the normal standards of Homeric warfare he has every right to do so. Agamemnon by his action forfeits any claim he may have had. But it is lamentable that a youth so generous should so ignore the claim of others who have fought with him as friends, and need his help. We understand his deep resentment, even his desire to teach the Greeks a lesson, till they honour him. But this appeal for their defeat with shame and slaughter shocks us, and the poet meant it should. Even his mother, Thetis, though she promises to intercede with Zeus, and keeps her promise, softens the request as any careful mother would.

After a lovely episode, in which Odysseus takes Chryseis to her father, and with sacrifice and song placates Apollo, Achilles still sits, nursing wrath.

He sat and nursed his wrath beside the swift ships on the shore,
Frequenting not the glorious Assembly any more,
Nor going out to war, though he longed incessantly
To be back among the fighters and to hear the battlecry.
    But Thetis, well remembering her much-loved son's request,
In a misty vapour dress'd,
Rising from the waters, climbed Olympus, where, alone,
The keen-eyed son of Cronos sat, aloof from all the rest;
The highest height of many-valed Olympus was His throne.
    She went to Him and sat by Him, in supplication laid
Her right hand on His bearded chin, her left hand on His knee,
And very earnestly
To Zeus, the son of Cronos, the King of gods, she prayed:
    Zeus, honour me my son, for he is doomed to die so soon . . .
Give honour to my son, I say, and let the Trojans win the day

Until the Greeks atone,
Acknowledging the honour and the glory of my son.[1]

That is very different from a prayer for their defeat with shame and slaughter.

She spoke. The Cloud-Compeller gave no answer to the prayer,
But sat in silence a long time, while Thetis, clinging there,
Moved not, and thus at length a second time His answer sought.
   Promise me in truth, and by thy Nod confirm it so,
Or else refuse me—thou art not afraid—that I may know
My godhead and my honour in thine eyes a thing of nought.
Strangely moved, the Cloud-Compeller, Zeus the Lord replied:
Bitter work indeed! You will be setting me at odds
With Hera, who, provoking me, right bitterly will chide,
Since even now she rails on me, alleging to the gods,
I am favouring the Trojans and am fighting on their side.
   Go thou apart, lest Hera note our conference. I swear,
By my own head I promise it. These things shall be my care;
And whatsoever thing my Nod hath once confirmed, no other god
May question. When my brows are bent
The word remains, nor can deceive, nor lack accomplishment.
   He spoke and His dark eyebrows bent. On the immortal head
The ambrosial curls rippled, and all Olympus quaked in dread.[1]

"These things shall be my care." What does that promise mean? It is a mystery no mortal man, nor any other god than Zeus, not even Hera, Queen of Heaven, can solve. None can discern the high god's purpose till the hour and the event reveal it.

In the world of Homer, as of the Old Testament, a man's first act of Hubris breeds fresh mischief, and Infatuation follows. Security becomes his chiefest enemy. So it is now with Agamemnon.

[1] i, 488 ff., and especially 511–530.

So in a deeply tragic sense it is to be with the Zeus-loved Achilles.

Agamemnon dreams he will take Troy next day, and launches an attack, which we are sure must fail.

It fails, but not at first disastrously. In a long day of fighting and negotiation, the Trojans hold their own so well that the Greeks think it wise to take advantage of a truce, for burial of the dead, and build a wall about their camp. On a second day for many hours the fight is equal: [1]

In the morning, while the sacred day was waxing, they fought on,
And many a weapon found its mark and many a man went down.
But when the Sun bestrode high heaven, the golden scales were
 set,
And Zeus the Father put in both a doom disconsolate
Of Death, one for the Greeks, and for the Trojan horsemen one.

He grasped the centre of the beam: He weighed each Destiny:
And lo! the Greek scale sank to earth, the Trojan mounted high.
Then Zeus from Ida thundered, and a flash of fire He sped
Among the Greeks, who wondered, by pale fear discomfited.

The Greeks fight well and stubbornly, encouraged by Athena, then by Hera, but Zeus intervenes, and they are driven back to their camp in great confusion, while Hector follows, cutting off stragglers "like a hound that worries the beast it has pursued." The Trojans, now no longer the besieged but the besiegers, pass the night beside their watch-fires in the plain, and Hector gives an order that old men and boys should man the walls of Troy, and fires be lit to light the streets and so

[1] viii, 66–77.

prevent an ambush or an infiltration of the enemy
to the unguarded town.

Agamemnon, at a Council summoned in the
night, acknowledges his fault. "I was infatuated.
I will not deny it." [1] He sends a deputation to
Achilles, offering amends, imploring help.

It is too late. The young man's heart is
hardened. He has nursed resentment till it has
become a fixed obsession. In vain the skilled
diplomatist Odysseus urges every plea of common
sense and of self-interest. In vain the loyal Ajax
shows, by his demeanour more than words, how
deeply his young friend's rejection of the claim of
friendship hurts. In vain old Phoenix, who has
loved and served Achilles since he was a child,
reminds him: "You were once a babe, Achilles,
and you needed help. Your friends are praying to
you. Prayers are daughters of high Zeus, and men
reject them at their peril. Beware. Infatuation
breeds disaster." [2]

No, I will not yield. They are to suffer more before I help.

We have reached the turning-point of the whole
tragic movement which began with Agamemnon's
Hubris, his rejection of the old man's ransom for
his child. Achilles has been offered fair amends,
and has refused. Prayers are the daughters of high
Zeus, and he rejects them.

So the fight goes on until at last the Greek

[1] ix, 116. [2] ix, 302 ff.

defeat becomes a rout. Deeply moved, Patroclus stood before his friend in tears, and Achilles, when he saw it, pitied him. "Why do you weep, Patroclus, like a little girl who runs beside her mother, plucking at her skirt, delaying her, however much she hurries, looking up at her in tears, to make her pick her up and comfort her?" ". . . Why are you so distressed? Have you bad news from home? . . . Surely it cannot be that you are grieving for the plight of these Achaeans, who are suffering for their own fault?" Then the magnificent appeal of Patroclus to the claim of friendship and to his friend's own honour, and at last the reluctant, fatal, half-consent. "Yes, you yourself may go. You may lead our men to the rescue. I cannot. Wear my armour. The very sight of that will turn the battle. But I beg you, come back safely. Do not go too far."

Patroclus takes the field. At the first sight of him the Trojans waver. Fighting brilliantly, he kills Sarpedon, a very gallant gentleman, the son of Zeus himself. Sarpedon's time has come. Though Zeus rains tears of blood in sorrow for his child, neither for him nor Hector or Achilles, can Zeus cancel destiny. That indeed is the secret of heroic courage: that is why Sarpedon, earlier in the battle, told his friend Glaucus:

Dear man, if by avoiding this one battle, you and I
For ever should escape old age; if we should never die;
I should not fight among the first, nor would I bid you stand
Foremost in the front of war; but since on every hand

Ten thousand fates of chilly death lurk waiting anyhow,
Which no man living can avoid or counter, let us go,
To see if we win glory or give glory to the foe.[1]

Sarpedon falls, and Patroclus, flushed with triumph, presses on, caution forgotten. For a time success continues. Then at last Hector kills him, strips him of Achilles' armour, and in momentary triumph, boasts of victory. Over the fallen body of Patroclus Greeks and Trojans fight, but Zeus sends darkness on the field. "Zeus, if thou wilt destroy," cried Ajax, "slay us in the light"; and Zeus sent light where they were fighting, but the rest of the field was dark. Achilles did not know his friend was dead.[2]

Achilles did not know. But when at last Antilochus brought the news, he fell to the ground prostrate, and lifted up his voice in self-contempt and anguish. Thetis heard, and came to him. "My son, why do you weep? Has not Zeus granted all your prayer?"

Mother, all these things indeed hath Zeus accomplishéd
But what profit have I in these things. My friend is dead,
And I did not help . . . [3]

He knows now that, compared with friendship and with loyalty to friends, the praise of men which he called "honour," is as nothing. But he has yet more to suffer and to learn.

The old grudge quite forgotten, he has now one

[1] xii, 322–328.   [2] xvii, 645 ff.   [3] xviii, 79 ff.

thought, one only, to avenge his friend. "I must kill Hector. I no longer wish to live unless I kill him." Thetis reminds him, "Your own death must follow soon." "What matter? Let it come ... I would that Strife might perish from the earth and heaven. A quarrel is so sweet at first, but now ... I will die when my time comes, but first kill Hector and win glory." [1] He is still the same man with a new, more terrible obsession. "Wait at least until the morning," Thetis pleads; "then I will come again and bring you armour."

He waits, and in the early morning Thetis comes again, bringing the armour and the shield which the lame craftsman-god has made for him in pity for them both. "I wish," the god has said, "I wish I could as surely save your child from death as he shall surely have fine armour"; and he made it fine although he knew it could not save him. He embossed the shield in bronze and tin and precious gold and silver with a pattern of the life Achilles, as a prince of Phthia, might have had if he had not preferred to fight and die at Troy. He put on it the Earth and Sea and Sky, the Sun, the Stars and Ocean. He put on it scenes from the life of men in peace and war, marriages, harvest-home and ploughing, vintage, song and dancing; but in the background also strife and sorrow, sudden fear and death. Clad in this armour, carrying this shield, Achilles goes into the fight with

[1] xviii, 107 ff.

the knowledge that, when Hector falls, his own death will soon follow.[1]

At that moment when, as Andrew Lang has said, "the final strife is set" between these mortal heroes, Zeus, in a full Assembly of the gods, "from Apollo and Athene to the nymphs of rivers, well-heads and grassy meadows," makes the pronouncement which reveals the depth and the sincerity of Homer's tragic intuition. The Father pities even when he cannot save. "I care for them," says Zeus. "They matter to me, though they perish." He has not forgotten how he said to Thetis, when she pleaded with him for the "honour" of her son, "These things shall be my care."[2]

Achilles fights more brilliantly, more ruthlessly than ever, and, as he fights, the new obsession grows on him till it becomes a blinding lust for blood. He is near madness, when at last he meets and kills his noble enemy, and, having killed him, shamefully maltreats his body. In the sight of men and gods it is an outrage.

Young, generous, impulsive, he has come to this. But it is not the end. The plan of Zeus, the secret purpose of his promise, is not yet fulfilled.

[1] xviii, 463-608. For a more detailed discussion both of the Shield and of the function of its symbolism in the whole poem I may perhaps be allowed to refer the reader to my book *The Pattern of the Iliad* (Methuen), 1922.

[2] xx, 21. Andrew Lang, *The World of Homer* (Longmans), 1910, p. 120.

Day after day, still bent on wreaking futile vengeance even on the dead, still tortured by remorse,
Achilles has to suffer. Then, slowly, very slowly,
he returns to sanity. At last, worn out with the
long agony, he falls asleep, and in a dream he
seems to hear his friend Patroclus speaking.
"Have you forgotten me, Achilles? Bury me
quickly. Let me pass the gates of Hades." Then
the spirit of his friend, in life so kind, so wise,
awakes the memories of early youth and of a lesson
which Patroclus learnt from sad experience. "We
were reared together at your home in Phthia,
whither I was brought, a little child, because of a
fatal killing. I had killed the son of Amphidamas,
not meaning it, in childishness—in a fit of anger
about knuckle-bones. Your father welcomed me
and reared me and made me your servant. Let
one urn receive the ashes of us both." [1]

That is Homer's comment on the tragedy and
the futility of war. The vision is a prelude to the
music of the sequel when Achilles comes to his
right mind.

That is not yet. He has not yet learnt his
lesson. He sacrifices at Patroclus' pyre twelve
Trojan prisoners, and cries, after that evil deed,
"Give you good greeting, Patroclus. I fulfil for
you my promise. Here are twelve sons of the
great-hearted Trojans, all consumed with you by
fire. But Hector I shall give, not to the fire, but
to the dogs."

[1] xxiii, 69 ff.

Nevertheless at the funeral games which follow there is more than formal courtesy, a touch of gentleness which moves us and reminds us of his friend.

Night falls. Achilles cannot sleep, and in the morning he resumes the miserable, futile rite of vengeance. Day after day he fastens Hector's body to his chariot and drags it round Patroclus' tomb, then leaves it naked in the dust. Apollo saves it from corruption. The gods are full of indignation and of pity. They protest to Zeus. Can he ignore the outrage? Finally Apollo, scandalized and angry, threatens he himself will snatch away the body from Achilles and so make an end.

Zeus intervenes. "No, I will send for Thetis. She shall go to him. This is the honour that I give him—of his own free will, he shall relent." So for the last time Thetis comes to help her son, to touch his heart with reverence for Zeus, and bring him back the human pity which Apollo says he has quite lost.

Then Iris goes to Troy for Priam. "I am a messenger from Zeus. He bids you go and ransom Hector." Hecuba implores her husband not to go, but he replies, "It was told me by a god, and I will go. Gladly I will let Achilles kill me, if I first have held my dear son in my arms." He passes through the enemy lines by night, escorted, though he does not know it, by a god, Hermes, "as beautiful as a young prince." They reach Achilles' hut. The door is opened by the god, and Priam enters.

The music of the closing scene resolves in wonder and in pity the discord sounded first when Agamemnon turned away an old man, pleading for his child. That theme was heard again on muted strings when Phoenix bade Achilles yield to Prayers, the daughters of high Zeus, and the young man refused. Now, at the sight of Priam, kneeling at his feet, Achilles marvels at his courage, and listens to his prayer. "Remember, son of Peleus, your own father." Both remember. Priam thinks of Hector, and Achilles thinks of Peleus, who said, when he set out for Troy—"My child, Athena, if she will, and Hera, will give you victory. But keep in check your passion. Loving kindness is far better. Cease from strife, the mischief-maker, that the Argives, young and old, may honour you the more." [1] So now Achilles says, "I look on you and think of my own father," and grants the old man's prayer.

Thus the mysterious promise is fulfilled, "These things shall be my care." Achilles has the honour to become, of his free choice, a man again, and capable of mercy and of understanding. His honour has been saved "in the fulfilment of the Will of Zeus" and through the loving ministry of Thetis: but also by the memory of his friend's loving-kindness and his father's wisdom. Such memories were working in him, though he did not know it, when he cried to Thetis: "Would that Strife might perish from the earth."

[1] ix, 254 ff.

THE SCAEAN GATE

SOME thirty years ago a party of Hellenic travellers, while on their way to Troy, received this message: "May Troy look its best, and when you stand where Helen stood, may a romantic haze pervade the rubbish-heaps and mudflats." Presently we looked out on the Trojan plain from a high crumbling tower, a mass of broken masonry, and did not much care whether archaeologists identify it with the Scaean Gate. For us it was the place where Helen talked with Priam, where Hector met his wife, and where a child, "in beauty like a star," shrank back in terror from the sight of his dear father in grim battle-gear. It was the place where Priam tore his hair and wept, and Hecuba bared her breast in vain to Hector, imploring him to come within the walls for safety.

All this we seemed to see. Then, looking out across the plain, "Yonder," we thought, "sits young Achilles, idle and unhappy." That was perhaps to some of us the most moving thought of all. But then we thought again of Hector and we marvelled at the genius of the poet who, in contrast to the tragedy of youth's ungoverned passion, set a hero, steadfast and true-hearted, fighting to the death for a lost cause.

Steaming again past Troy on that stifling

69

summer afternoon, we saw what Homer must have seen when he imagined Ajax fighting to defend the body of Patroclus. Over the land a sudden storm gathered and broke, though we at sea were still in brilliant sunshine. On the plain gross darkness fell. But sheets and forks of lightning lit one patch, a little village, white against the murk. Then we remembered how the hero cried "Zeus, if thou wilt destroy, destroy us in the light"; and Zeus shed light upon them where they strove, though the rest of the field was dark. Achilles did not know.

Thanks to the Muse, Troy lives although Troy fell. In spring Mount Ida, robed by hyacinth and crocus in fresh gold and purple, tells again the story of the mating of the Queen of Heaven with her consort, Father of all gods and men. In winter, when the trickle of Scamander swells to a fierce flood, men say, "The river-god is angry with Achilles." But Achilles sleeps, and Hector sleeps, unless the Muse awakes them, as she did for Rupert Brooke when, in the sick-bay of a warship off the Dardanelles, he heard the guns, and wrote

> They say Achilles in the darkness stirred,
> And Hector, his old enemy,
> Moved the great shades that were his limbs. They heard
> More than Olympian thunder on the sea.

Troy lives. Let us take our stand again upon the battlements and watch.

What is that heap of ruined masonry far out

into the plain? What is that hillock overgrown with scrub? Shall we take a spade and dig? First let us look and listen. We may hear and see what Homer heard and saw.

The Greeks were marching. Like a fire they swept the plain,
And Earth beneath the feet of that great army groaned amain.

Agamemnon's grand offensive had begun.

But a wind-swift messenger from aegis-bearing Zeus,
Iris, to the Trojan people brought the bitter news.
They were gathered in assembly, young and old, at Priam's gate,
Gathered there for high debate, and very near the goddess came
To speak to them. She took on her the voice of Priam's son,
Polites was his name, and very swiftly he could run,
And he trusted in his swiftness. As a sentinel he sat
At the monument of ancient Aisuetes . . .

Yes, we see. That mass of stone was once the tomb of a wise counsellor of Troy, the father of Antenor, a good man who counselled peace.

At the monument of ancient Aisuetes there he sat
To watch for every movement from the camp of the Achaeans
And give warning of the same; in his likeness Iris came
And spoke to Priam. *Sir*, she said,
Incessantly you hold debate,
As of old, in time of peace. But war is at your gate.
Many battles have I seen, but I have never seen before
So great a multitude of men advancing in the plain,
As numerous as forest leaves or as the sand on the sea-shore . . .
Hector, on you I lay this charge . . .
　　　　　　　　　　　She spoke, and Hector, since he knew
It was a goddess spoke, obeyed.[1]

That is how Homer introduces Hector, the defender of the cause of Troy, the noblest hero of

[1] *Il.* ii, 780 ff.

them all. And that is how he tells us, Hector was a man who instantly obeyed the call of duty. What he heard was the voice of a young citizen, the sentinel Polites. But he knew "it was a goddess spoke"; it was a call from heaven. Such things did happen in the world of Homer. When Athena, for example, came to young Telemachus to put some spirit in his heart, she took the form of Mentes, his own father's friend, and talked with him as Mentes. When she took her leave, he knew "it was a god," and walked among the suitors with new life in him, "a godlike man." [1]

A poet sings, and he believes the Muse has taught him. A prophet speaks, and he believes the word is given him by Zeus or by Apollo. A friend speaks to a friend, and the word helps or even saves him from disaster. "It was a god who spoke," they say. Euripides himself, however sceptical he was about the gods, however critical of some, at least, of their alleged activities, made Helen cry in Egypt when she met and recognized her husband,

> Heaven's mercy, it is a god when lovers meet. [2]

Is that the truth, we ask ourselves, or somehow "like the truth"?

She spoke, and Hector, since he knew it was a goddess spoke, obeyed.

He broke up the Assembly, and at once the people flew
To arms, and all the footmen and the horsemen rush'd to battle,
very loud the hubbub grew.

[1] *Od.* i, 322–324.   [2] *Helena,* 560.

Now before the city gate a hillock rises from the plain,
Standing clear in open ground, a landmark, known to me
As Bataia, Thistle-Brake but by the gods immortal hight
Myrrhina's Mound, because a fair
Fleet-footed maid lies buried there.
There the Trojans and allies were gathered in their companies
And mustered for the fight.[1]

"The Commander of the Trojans was great Hector, Priam's son." But who was Myrrhina— Myrtle? A fair Amazon who died in battle? A dancing-girl? Who knows? She died, and everyone forgot, except the gods. They know. They care.

Agamemnon launches his attack, and the two armies march, the Trojans noisily,

With clamour, like the cry
Of birds who fill the front of heaven with tumult as they fly,
Like the trumpeting of cranes . . .
But the Achaean soldiers marched in silence, breathing might,
Eager in their hearts to help their comrades in the fight.[2]

So, just perceptibly, we are reminded that Achilles, who should be the bravest and the first, is absent, "nursing wrath." But the contrast between Greek and Trojan is designed by Homer to prepare us first for Hector's stern rebuke to Paris, then for Helen's wavering between the charm of Paris, "in his beauty like a god," and the memory of home and of her husband, "to the god of battle dear."

[1] *Il.* ii, 808–816.   [2] iii, 2–3, 9–10.

73

The marching hosts were very near each other. From the van
Of the Trojans, out there strode, in his beauty like a god,
Alexander, and he challenged the best warriors of Argos
To meet him then and there, and to fight him man to man.[1]

Menelaus, like a hungry lion who has found his
prey, leapt on the challenger, who instantly withdrew, and Hector cried:

False, fatal Paris, woman-chaser, beautiful you are,
But I wish that you had died unwed, or never had been born;
That indeed were better far, and I would it had been so,
Than to ruin us and live a thing of scorn as now you do.
You, being what you are, took ship, mustered a trusty crew,
Sailed overseas, and, mingling with strange people, came again
With a woman in your train, very beautiful, to be
A kinswoman for fighting men, a fell calamity
To your father and your city and the Trojan people too,
A joy to all your enemies, and a foul shame to you.
  And yet you would not dare to meet the soldier Menelaus,
To the god of battle dear. You would very soon have known
What kind of man it is whose wife you handle as your own.
In the dust before his feet, little profit would you have
Of your harp, your hair, your beauty, all that Aphrodite gave.
We Trojans are too scrupulous. The wrong that you have done
Should long ago have wrapped you in the traitor's shroud of
      stone.[1]

Homer's charity and human sympathy embraces
even Paris.

Prince Alexander, godlike in his beauty, thus replied:
Hector, the reproach is just. You have the right to chide.
Your heart is hard. As a sharp axe cuts cleanly through the wood,
Aiding a man's strength and skill who labours to make good
A timber for a ship, your dauntless spirit serves your will.
Taunt me not with the gifts of love by golden Aphrodite given;
What the gods give none may refuse, though none of his own will
      would choose,
The glorious gifts of heaven.

[1] iii, 15 ff., 39–75, 97–100.

You wish to see me fight? Then bid the Trojans take their ease
And the Greeks, and set me in the field to fight alone
For Helen and her treasure with the soldier Menelaus,
To the god of battle dear; and whichever shall appear
The victor and the better man shall keep what he has won;
And the rest of you shall swear an oath of loyalty and peace,
And you shall dwell in deep-loamed Troy, and they shall cross the
    seas
To the land of lovely women and the pastured steeds of Greece.[1]

This man's will is weak, and yet he has a gift of imagination Hector lacks. The touch of obstinacy which he sees in Hector makes the hero great, but also vulnerable. Presently Andromache will tell her husband, "Your own spirit will destroy you in the end."

As for Helen, the last words of Paris are enough to show us why she finds him irresistible. But Menelaus' answer, when he hears the challenge, has a dignity which makes us understand why, in the sequel, she moves away in sympathy towards her home and husband:

Listen to my word as well. There is not anyone
So much aggrieved as I, but I am minded to have done
With this war of Greeks and Trojans. You have suffered far
    too long
In a quarrel which is mine, though Alexander did the wrong.[1]

The challenge is accepted and preparations for a truce and duel are begun.

Then Iris took the news to white-armed Helen, putting on
The likeness of the fairest of the daughters of King Priam,
Her kinswoman Laodice, whom prince Antenor's son,
Helicaon, cherished as his wife . . .[2]

---

[1] iii, 15 ff., 39–75, 97–100.   [2] iii, 120–145.

Antenor is a counsellor who stands for peace. He rescued Menelaus and Odysseus from mob violence, when they came upon an embassy from Greece before the war. So Iris, in the likeness of Laodice, sought Helen.

> She found her in the palace hall, where at the loom she wrought
> A rich and royal tapestry, embroidering thereon
> The trials which the knights of Troy and brazen-clad Achaeans
> Suffered at the war-god's hand, and suffered for her sake . . . [1]

She told her: "Paris and your husband are to fight for you. Whichever wins will claim you as his wife."

> So the goddess spoke. In Helen's heart she lit a flame
> Of longing for her husband and her parents and her home.
> She veiled herself in a bright veil of linen finely spun,
> And, delicately weeping, passed swiftly from the room—
> Not alone: two serving-maids were with her . . . [1]

Thus attended, Helen made her way to the city wall—

> And there above the Scaean Gate the elders of the city sat . . .
> Old age had stopped their fighting now, but very well they knew
> How to talk, as crickets will, that perch upon a bough
> And chirp with lily voices; so those elders of the Trojans
> Sat upon the battlements, and so they talked, and so,
> At the sight of Helen as towards the tower she sped,
> One to another, whispering the wingéd words, they said:
> *None can blame the Trojans and the stoutly-greaved Achaeans*
> *If for such a woman's sake they suffer grief so long:*
> *She is strangely like in beauty to the goddesses immortal:*
> *Even so, let her begone . . .* [2]

All these old men vaguely wish that they could see the last of Helen. One of them, Antenor, will

[1] iii, 120–145.   [2] 145–160.

presently find courage to demand in public her surrender. For the moment Priam and Antenor try to help her and relieve her heart by leading her to speak about her husband. With that purpose Priam asks "Who is that mighty chieftain?" though of course he knows quite well. Homer's old men may seem, like Nestor, artless, vague, inconsequent. They have the subtle sympathy and courage of ripe age.

> So they said. But Priam called to Helen. *Come to me,*
> *Hither, my belovéd child. Sit by my side, and see*
> *Your former husband, folk and friends. It is not you I blame*
> *For the tears that we have shed in this war with the Achaeans,*
> *But the gods from whom it came . . .* [1]

Exquisitely kind, but Priam is the King of Troy. The war is partly his responsibility.

> *Now tell me, can you name*
> *That great Achaean brave, so tall, so gallant? Who is he?*
> *Others are taller by a head. But I have never seen*
> *A finer gentleman than he, nor any with a mien*
> *And presence more majestical. I think he is a King.*

Of course he knows. Of course she knows he knows.

> Said Helen, answering:
> *Dear father, how I wish, as I love you and revere,*
> *How I wish that when I first came hither with your son,*
> *Left my bridal-chamber, my acquaintance, and the dear*
> *Companionship of girls I loved, and one who was my own*
> *Daughter—how I wish it might have been my lot to die.*
> *It was not so, and therefore now I languish, weeping bitterly.*
> *As for your question, I will answer thus. The lordly son*

---

[1] iii, 161–244.

Of Atreus is the man you mean, the noble Agamemnon,
A good king and strong soldier. He
Was husband's brother once to me,
A thing of shame and infamy if ever there was one.

With a delicacy which some modern parents well
might envy, Priam talks as if at random for awhile,
to cover her distress. Then, when he thinks it
time to "look again, and see," he picks on Odysseus.
His question and comparison of that broad-chested
chief to a ram, pacing up and down the lines of
sheep are cheerful, lighter in tone than what went
before. Helen answers briefly. She is still much
moved.

Helen, sprung from Zeus, replied, That is Laertes' son,
Odysseus, who is known as the man of many a wile.
Though he was reared in Ithaca, a rugged country, he
Is master of all shrewd designs and every sort of guile.

That gives Antenor, the diplomatist, his cue. He
talks about Odysseus, but contrives to give the
wife a picture of her husband, thus:

Lady, that is true, for this same glorious Odysseus
Came as an ambassador upon your business here
With the soldier Menelaus, to the god of battle dear.
I entertained them in my hall. I gave them both good cheer,
And I learnt to know the favour and the mind of both the men.
*   Now, when all the people stood in the Assembly, Menelaus*
Towered with his broad shoulder over all, but when the twain
Took their seats, Odysseus was the more majestical.
And when they wove their counsel into words before the folk,
If Menelaus spoke, though he was the younger man,
His words, though few, ran clear and true, and very well they ran.
But when the man of many wiles, Odysseus, took his stand,
He never moved his staff at all, but held it in his hand,
Like one who had not understood. He never raised his hand,

But peered at us beneath his brows. Indeed you might have said
The man was stubborn or a fool. But when words came at last,
Like winter snowflakes, thick and fast, and when Odysseus hurled
The great voice from that breast, he had no equal in the world.

So subtly the old statesman plays his hand, reminding her of her tall, honest husband.

Then Priam looked for the third time, and, seeing Ajax, said:
Who is that Achaean brave, so gallant and so tall
That he towers above the others, head and shoulders over all?
Helen of the trailing robe, fairest of women, said—
That is the huge Ajax, the defence of the Achaeans,
And yonder is Idomeneus . . .

Is it so surprising, as Leaf thought, that Ajax is dismissed by Helen in one line, and Diomed omitted altogether? Must we suppose, as he suggested, that Idomeneus has here "supplanted the more famous heroes"? From Homer's point of view, what praise can be more suitable for Ajax than this one great line? So in the *Catalogue* his greatness and his character are summed up in one line: "Ajax brought from Salamis twelve ships." As for Helen, what is Diomed to her? In the *Iliad* he has yet to prove himself a hero. Mention of him here would be irrelevant and careless. Homer knows his trade. His Helen takes small interest in "huge Ajax," and dismisses him, with a phrase which says more in his favour than a dozen lines, and talks about her husband's friend. It helps her. When she heard about the entertainment of the embassy in Troy, her mind went back to the old days in Sparta, when, as Menelaus' wife, she entertained his friends. So now she says:

79

That is the huge Ajax, the defence of the Achaeans,
And Idomeneus from Crete, like a god in majesty,
Stands yonder with his captains. We were often visited
By Idomeneus from Crete, and he was welcomed with good cheer
In our home by Menelaus, to the god of battle dear.

Menelaus was himself away in Crete, on a visit to Idomeneus, when Paris came to Sparta. So the perfect episode draws to its close. Having named her husband, Helen says:

But now, although I see among these glancing-eyed Achaeans,
Many other captains I could recognize and name,
Two who should be marshalling their men I cannot see,
Castor, the proud horseman, and the boxer Polydeuces,
My own brothers, by the self-same mother. Can it be,
My brothers would not come from Lacedaemon, their dear home,
Or came in the swift ships but will not fight, because they fear
The reproaches they may hear, and the whisper of ill fame
For my dishonour and my shame? So Helen said, but they
Beneath the fostering earth in their dear Lacedaemon lay.

In the plain the oaths are taken for truce, and sacrifices made by Priam and Antenor for the one part, Agamemnon and Odysseus for the other. The lists are set and the two rivals fight, but Paris, at the moment of defeat, is snatched away by Aphrodite.

Like a goddess, easily, she snatched the man from jeopardy,
And, wrapt in mist, she set him down in the dim fragrant bridal-
room.

There follows a companion picture in which Helen's heart, so lately yearning for her husband, turns again to Paris.[1]

[1] iii, 383–447.

Aphrodite went to summon Helen, whom she found
On the high tower still, with many Trojan women round;
She plucked at Helen's fine-spun, fragrant veil, and then she
  spoke
In the likeness of an ancient dame, a worker in fine wool,
Who had served the Queen in Sparta, so that Helen's heart was
  full
Of love for her, and that was why the shining Aphrodite took
Her likeness when she spoke.

  Come this way, this way, she said. *Alexander calls you home,*
Beautiful, in raiment rare, you will find him waiting there,
On the couch elaborate, in the bridal room;
Not a soldier, you would say, who has fought his man to-day,
But a dancer going to the dancing-place, or one
Resting when the dance is done.

  So she spoke, and at the word anger stirred in Helen's breast,
Then she looked again, and lo! the goddess stood confessed
By the glory of her bosom and her throat and shining eyes,
So that Helen marvelled, and addressed her in this wise:

  Out on you to cheat me so! I see it is your will
To spirit me away again among the towns of men,
Far away to Phrygia or beautiful Moeonia,
Wherever in the world you have some favourite to please,
Since Menelaus has this day defeated Alexander,
And means to take me home in spite of all my shame to Greece.
Go to! Renounce the paths of heaven. Get you to Alexander,
Nor ever more retrace your steps to climb Olympus' hill,
But sit with him, be grieved for him, watch over him, until
He takes you for his wife, or for his slave. I will not go
To serve his pleasure. It would be a shameful thing to do,
And all the Trojan women would reproach me for it too.
It is strange to suffer so.

If it be true, as Mr. F. L. Lucas says, that
Homer's charity is more than Christian, that is a
reproach to us. The woman wavers. She is
fighting still to keep her thought of Menelaus
clear. But she will go to Paris. It will need no
miracle to take her back.

Then shining Aphrodite, wrathfully replied:
Wretch, provoke me not, or I will leave you in your pride,
And will prove my hate as bitter as my love for you was great.
I shall stir up strife again. These Trojans and Achaeans
Still shall suffer hate and pain, and you shall die disconsolate.

She spoke, and Helen, child of Zeus, became afraid.
Silently, unnoticed by the Trojan dames, she sped
Homeward, veiled in shining linen, by the goddess led.
So they reached the lordly palace, Alexander's home,
And her maidens hastened quickly to their labour at the
    loom,
But the fairest among women sought the high-roofed bridal-
    room.

Then the smiling goddess, Aphrodite, placed a chair
Close at hand, for Helen's use, facing Alexander. There
Helen, the bright daughter of the aegis-bearer Zeus,
Sat, and with averted eyes railed on Paris in this wise:
You are home from battle then? I wish you had been slain
By the man who was my husband once, a mighty man of war.
You boasted, and you called yourself a better man by far,
And stronger with the spear, than the soldier Menelaus,
To the god of battle dear. Away! Go, challenge him again.
Go, stand in the encounter face to face with Menelaus,
To the god of battle dear. No, no! I counsel you, refrain;
For if heedlessly you match yourself with bright-haired Menelaus,
In the fight you may be slain. But Alexander thus replied:
Do not chide me, wife, so harshly. Menelaus, it is true,
Has beaten me to-day: he had Athena on his side:
But some day I shall win, for we have gods to help us too.
Let us to bed. Come, join your love with mine. In all my life
I was never yet so deep in love, not even on the day
When I carried you perforce away from your sweet Lacedaemon,
Nor even in our first embrace on rugged Cranaë,
Were love and sweet desire of love so masterful in me.

He spoke, and led the way to the bridal-bed, and she
Followed him as his wife.

We are delighted in the battle-scenes which
follow that Diomed wounds Aphrodite, and we
smile when she runs whimpering to tell her Father

she is hurt. It is just a scratch, and Athena's mockery is well deserved.[1]

Father Zeus, will you be angry with the word that I shall say?
It appears that Aphrodite has been trying to persuade
One of the fair-robed Achaean maids to run away
With a Trojan she holds dear, and, in caressing her,
She has pricked her finger on the lady's golden brooch, I fear.
So she spoke, and Zeus, the Father of all gods and mortals, smiled,
And bade the Golden Aphrodite come to him and said, *My child,*
Your gift is not for fighting. You will find it better far
To manage lovely marriages, which are your own affair,
And leave the business of the war to Ares and Athena's care.

So much for that delightful, irresponsible, pernicious plague. The battle in the plain goes on.

Presently Diomed meets and overthrows (Athena helping him) a far worse plague, the war-god Ares. The discomfiture of Aphrodite was, as we have seen, a sequel to the story of the mischief done by Helen's frailty. The overthrow of Ares is the signal for another set of Trojan scenes, in which the noblest soldier of them all is shown in converse, both with Helen, and with the two women who are dearest to him, and will suffer most, his mother and his wife.

Hector's heart, whatever Paris says, is not "of iron," though he sometimes talks as if it were. The *Iliad* is not a panegyric of the war-god, but a poet's true account of war, and what it does to men and women. Even in Hector, a great soldier and a noble gentleman, there are, as Mr. Gladstone

[1] v, 421–430.

noted, symptoms of an overstrain,[1] a sense of a
responsibility too heavy for him. If sometimes he
seems to lack imaginative sympathy, we understand. There are moments even when he seems
uncertain of himself—not clear about his duty—
save for this, that he must always fight for Troy.

Always? When Helenus, the prophet, bids him
leave the field, just at a time when things are going
badly for the Trojans, Hector instantly obeys, and,
though the poet makes no comment, scholiasts are
loud in their expression of surprise. A prophet is,
of course, a prophet. But is this the man who later
will defy a sign from Zeus himself? "One omen,
to defend the fatherland, is best." That splendid
cry is surely the more moving because normally
this man is overscrupulous, too sensitive to other
men's opinions. When the prophet says, "Get
you to Hecuba, and bid the women pray," he goes,
and yet, I think, he is uneasy. Anyhow, he tells
his men, "I go to bid the counsellors, the elders
and their wives, make supplication." That sounds
better somehow than "I go to Hecuba." Some
critics think his phrase is a survival, a fossil, from
a version of the tale in which a Trojan Council
really met. I can't believe it. Simply Hector,
speaking to his men, said that.

At the Scaean Gate the Trojan women met him,
and questioned him about their men. He sent
them all to pray.

[1] *Juventus Mundi*, xiv, 6, a deeply interesting analysis by Mr.
Gladstone of a character in some ways not unlike his own.

Then he came to Priam's palace, with its polished porticoes,
Gleaming, very beautiful, wherein were fifty chambers, close
To one another, built of polished stone, for the repose
Of Priam's sons with their dear wives . . .

The stillness of the place is in sharp contrast with the din of battle.

There his mother met him,[1] and she said, *Why have you come*
Home from the fierce battle? I suppose those men of evil fame.
The sons of the Achaeans, in the fight about our city proved
Overwhelming, and it moved
Your heart to seek the citadel, and raise your hands to Zeus in
prayer?
Wait, and I will fetch sweet wine, that you may pour libation
there,
First to Zeus the Father and the other gods, and then
Drink yourself. The wine will do you good. It gives men strength
again,
When they are spent, as you are spent, with fighting for your men.

If Homer makes no comment, Hecuba makes hers.

So she spoke, and Hector of the shining helmet answered her:
Mother, offer me no honeyed wine, which might impair
My strength and cause me to forget my courage. No, I should not
dare
To pour the flaming wine for Zeus with unwashed hands. It is not
thus,
With filth and blood befouled, a man should make his prayer to
Zeus.

Then he bids his mother fetch a precious robe, "the robe you value most," as a peace-offering for Pallas:

Get you to Athena's shrine, and I will go my way
To summon Paris, though I know not if he will obey.
How I wish the earth would gape and swallow him. I swear,
If I could see him safely dead, my soul would be set free from care.

[1] vi, 242–295.

85

We are not to ask, said Wilamowitz, whether such a speech would jar on Hecuba. Homer has not the dramatist's conception of a dialogue. I wonder. In real life such things as this do happen. Sons do sometimes say to mothers "How I hate my brother. How I wish that he were dead"—and mothers make no answer.

> *If I saw him dead, my soul would be set free from care,*
> He told her . . . and she went to the dim fragrant room
> Where many treasured robes were laid, the fabric of the loom,
> By womenfolk of Sidon made; and Paris from Sidonia,
> Godlike in his beauty, when he travelled the wide seas
> With highborn Helen, brought them home. The fairest among these
> Hecuba chose, to be Athena's gift.

The robe she treasured most was that son's gift, whom Hector has wished dead. Are we so sure that Homer did not understand?

Hector takes his leave and goes to summon Paris from the wondrous house he built with the best builders that there were in Troy.

> He found him in his chamber, busy with his gear . . .
> And when he saw him thus, reproached him bitterly, and cried:
> *How strange you are. This pique you entertain is no good thing . . .*[1]

This pique you entertain? After the language Hector used to Hecuba it seems too mild. No doubt it is, but Helen is in the room. Hector is acquainted with the etiquette of epic fighting, by which even heroes like Achilles can withdraw, if satisfaction for a grievance is refused them. So he

---

[1] vi, 325–368.

lets the man down lightly; saving Helen's presence, far too lightly. Paris, of course, accepts the situation.

Hector, the reproach is just, You have the right to chide.
Listen, I will tell you. Understand. It was not pique,
Nor any indignation that I felt against the Trojans,
But a mood I was too weak
To resist, a mood of grief. My wife was even now
Gently and persuasively suggesting I should go,
And I myself agree. Wait a moment for me here;
I will be putting on my gear—or rather, go ahead,
And I will follow presently. The shining-helmeted
Hector said nothing. Helen spoke. With honeyed words, she
    said:
Brother of me, child of shame and mischief-maker that I am,
How I wish that on the day my mother brought me from the womb,
A hurricane had swept me to the mountains or the sea,
To be whelmed beneath the waves before these things had come to me.
Or, since the gods decreed it thus, and brought these evil things to
    pass,
I wish my husband were a man who knew what indignation was,
A better man, who felt his own dishonour. Such unstable wit
Must still be shifting, and a man must pay the price of it.
  Brother, pray come in. Be seated here. There is not one
So beset with trouble for my shameful sake, and for the wrong
By Alexander first begun. Zeus laid an evil doom
On both of us, that we might be in generations yet to come
Remembered as a theme for song.
  He answered her and said, *Nay, Helen, though it show your love*
Do not ask me to be seated. Your persuasion will not move
My spirit, for I long to help the Trojans in their need.
They miss me. Rouse your husband. He had better make good speed
To overtake me in the town. I have to see my own
People first, before I go—my wife and little son,
Because indeed I cannot know if I shall come to them again,
Or if the gods will lay me low this day, by some Achaean slain.

If Helen's presence made the hero much more courteous to Paris than he had intended, did not the sight of her among her women make him suddenly decide he must go home to see his wife? He hurried to the house. She was not there. At a mere rumour of bad news, a servant says, she ran to the walls "like a madwoman"—though we doubt the accuracy of her phrase, because she adds, her mistress took the nurse and baby with her. Anyhow Hector traverses the town again, and at the Scaean Gate he finds his wife.[1]

She ran to meet him, and a serving-maid was with her, on whose breast
Lay a child, a tender babe, with gentle thoughts, at rest,
Hector's well-belovéd son; in beauty like a star he shone;
Scamandrios, as Hector called him, but the people called the boy
Astyanax, because his father was the sole defence of Troy.
    Hector smiled, and watched his son in silence. But Andromache
Wept, and coming close to him, she took his hand and said, *My friend,*
Your own spirit will destroy you in the end.

If she loses him, she tells him, she will have no comfort left.

I have no father and no gracious mother. Both are dead.
Bright Achilles slew my father, when he sacked and overthrew
Our city in Cilicia, high-gated Thebes; there he slew
Eetion, but spoiled him not: some scruple in his heart forbade;
And he burnt the King in his own shining armour clad,
Heaping a high mound for him, and mountain nymphs, the fair
Daughters of the aegis-bearer Zeus, have planted elm-trees there.
And my brothers—there were seven in our palace then—
All on that same day were slain . . .
But my mother, who was Queen under woody Plakos—she

---

[1] vi. 392–502.

Was brought with other spoil to Troy, and bright Achilles set
  her free
For precious ransom. But she died. The Queen of Archery,
Artemis, slew her in her father's hall. You, Hector, you alone
Are my father and my mother and my brother, and my own
Strong husband. Have some pity on my state. Stay with me
  here
On the tower of Troy . . . and bid the army take its stand
By the fig-tree, close at hand,
Where the town is most approachable, the ramparts most
  assailable.

That is impossible, we know, but it is hard for her
to bear, and we remember this refusal in the sequel
when Achilles, "pounced on Hector, like a hawk
upon a dove, and pursued him past the watch-
tower and the fig-tree," till they reached the springs
of the Scamander, "where the wives and daughters
of the Trojans washed their garments in the days
of peace, before Achaeans ever came."

Wife, these things are in my thoughts he says, *and yet I must press
  on,*
Fighting always for my father's honour and my own.
Well I know the day must come when sacred Troy is overthrown,
And Priam of the ashen spear, and Priam's people, must go down
In ruin. Yet my heart is not so full of grief for what must come
To Priam and the Trojans and to Hecuba, nor for the doom
Of my brothers, though so many and so noble, who must fall
In the dust before our enemies; I think not of them all
So much as of yourself, and of your tears, when you are led away
By some brazen-clad Achaean, who will rob you of the day
Of liberty . . . and dire necessity will rule your life,
*And you will weep, and men will see it, and will say "This is the
  wife*
Of Hector, the best warrior of these horse-taming Trojans,
In the days when men were fighting at the siege of Ilion."
*And you will have your grief renewed, and feel the need of such
  an one*
As I have been, for husband, to defend your liberty.

89

But may the heaped earth cover me, may I be dead, before the day
When I hear you cry for help, and see you dragged away.
With the word bright Hector stretched his arms to take the child,
But the boy shrank back upon his nurse's breast in fear,
And cried, because the sight of his dear father in that gear
Of bronze, and the great horse-hair plumes that waved so terribly
Above the helmet-crest, were fearful sights for him to see.

The loving father laughed, the gracious mother too,
And Hector took the helmet off, and with no more ado
Laid it on the ground before his feet, and left it there,
Gleaming. Then he kissed the boy, and tossed him in the air,
And to Zeus and all the other gods addressed his prayer—
Zeus and all ye other gods, vouchsafe that this my son
May prove, as I have proved, a man of note among the Trojans,
Not less excellent in might, a strong defence of Ilion.
Be it said of him some day, returning from the war,
"This man is better far than his father." May he bring to Troy
The blood-stained spoils of a foeman slain, and his mother's heart
*   have joy.*
So he spoke, and in his dear wife's arms he put the child.
She laid it on her fragrant breast, and through her tears she
    smiled,
Which her husband saw, and pitied her.

One thing remains. Before he leaves her for the
field, he tries to help her and to give her strength:

He said to her, *Dear woman, be not overmuch distressed.*
No man can send me down to death unless it be my doom.
No man once born into this world, no matter if he be
A brave man or a coward, can escape his destiny.
Get you to the house. Be busy with the distaff and the loom,
Intent on your own work, and keep the maidens busy too.
We men will think of war. It is the work we have to do,
The burden laid on every son of Troy, and most of all my own.

Bright Hector spoke, took up the crested helm, and put it on,
And his dear wife went her way homeward, ever and anon
Turning back, in tears, and when at length she reached the fair
Palace of man-slaying Hector, finding many maidens there,
Constrained them all to weep with her. Though Hector lived,
    they made
Lamentation in his house. *He will not come again*, they said,

He will not come in safety from the battle in the plain:
He will not be delivered from the hands of the Achaeans: he will
   never come again.

Hector and Paris go back to the field. The battle is renewed. Then, at a word again from Helenus, the prophet, Hector challenges whatever champion the Greeks may choose to single combat. The lot falls on Ajax, and the two men fight. They are well matched, and their encounter ends in a stalemate, with mutual courtesies and an exchange of gifts.

So Homer, using still his favourite device of formal patternings, contrasts and balances the talk of Helen at the Scaean Gate and the fight between her husband and her lover, with the meeting of Andromache and Hector and the duel between Hector and the hero who will bear the brunt of the defence for the Achaeans in the far more tragic battles of the sequel.

In the end, after the long agony of battle, Hector, flushed with his brief triumph, having fired the ships and killed Patroclus, and put on the armour of Achilles which Patroclus wore, will scornfully reject the counsel of the seer Polydamas, and so involve his army in disaster, and himself in the extremity for which he sees no remedy but death. He stands at last, defeated and at bay, before the Scaean Gate. His father weeps and tears his hair; his mother bares her breast, imploring pity for her motherhood. Andromache does

91

not know. She has obeyed her husband and has kept the house.

Even when Achilles dragged the body in the dust behind his car, she did not know.[1]

She had no news of Hector. No true messenger had come
To say her husband stayed without the gate. She sat at home,
Weaving in her inner chamber, working at the loom
On a web of purple, with a broidery elaborate
Of blossoms, and she called her fair-tressed maids and bade them set
A cauldron on the fire, because, when Hector came again,
He must have his bath. Poor fool, she knew not that the thought was vain.
Far from baths, by Pallas he was vanquished, by Achilles slain.

Suddenly she listened, and heard Hecuba's cry, and ran to the wall, and saw. She swooned, and the bridal-veil which was given her by Aphrodite on the day when Hector brought her home, fell from her head.

Finally, when at last the body of her husband is brought home, she, with two other women, leads the lamentation.[2]

They brought him to the palace hall; they laid him in a carven bed,
And bade the leaders of the dirge, the singers, take their stand
By the body, close at hand; and they began to sing
The lamentation for the dead, the women answering
With cries of grief, white-armed Andromache the first. She held the head
Of the man-slaying Hector between her hands, and said:
    Hector, you have gone from life too soon, and I am left alone,
A widow in your house, with a helpless babe, the one
Comfort born to us, your son. I think that even he
Will not live to manhood, for our city will be overthrown,

[1] xxii, 437–446.   [2] xxiv, 719–775.

Ravaged utterly, because her one defence is gone,
The sole protector of her wives and little children. Soon
The hollow ships will take them overseas, and I shall be
One of them, and you, my son, must either go with me
To toil at tasks unseemly and to serve some cruel king,
Or an Achaean chief will drag you to the battlements and fling
My baby to a fearful death, because you are the son
Of Hector, and your father slew his brother, or his own
Father, or his son—for many a brave Achaean fell
At great Hector's hands and bit the dust, for in that field of woe
Your father was a fighting-man, and dealt not gently with the foe.
So throughout our streets the people mourn thee, Hector, everywhere.
And thy parents have to bear a grief unspeakable for thee,
But my own legacy of sorrow is to know
This, that from your bed of death you did not stretch your arms to me
And say farewell, and speak one pregnant word for me to keep
In memory, and night and day remember it and weep.

Hecuba follows in an ecstasy of grief and pride as if in this extremity it has been given her to read, at least in part, the mystery of death:

Hector, dear to me as none of my other children were,
In your life the gods have shown you kindness, for they held you dear
And even now, though death has come, they kept you in their care.
Other sons indeed I had, whom swift Achilles made
His prisoners, but these across the sea unharvested
He sold to smoky Lemnos or to Samos or to Imbros,
But from you he took the life with the broad-edged bronze, and then
Dragged you round Patroclus' tomb again and yet again,
Though it could not bring him back the friend whom you had slain.
And lo! in spite of all my son is beautiful in death,
As fresh as dew, as fair as one
Whom Phoebus with his silver bow and kindly arrows visiteth.

93

Last Helen speaks:

Hector, dear to me as none of my husband's brothers, though
Paris, godlike in his beauty, brought me here, I know,
Would that I had died ere then—and is my husband now;
And, though since first I left my country twenty years have gone,
In all that time I have not heard one cruel or unseemly word
From you. If any of your sisters spoke to me,
Or any of your brothers' fair-robed wives, reproachfully,
Or your mother—for your father always was as good
As if I had been his own child—you checked them and you
        changed their mood
By your gracious spirit and your words of gentleness.
So I weep at once for you and for my own distress,
Because there is not anyone left in all wide Troy to be
My friend, and to be kind. They all shudder and shrink away
        from me.

So the woodcutters were sent up to the mountain
to fetch wood. The funeral pyre was built, and
kindled, and extinguished. Hector was buried
with all honour.

THE HOMECOMING TO
ITHACA

WHEN the reciters went from town to town, from
market-place to market-place in ancient Greece,
re-telling the familiar tales of Troy, it was their
custom, we are told, to robe themselves in crimson
for the *Iliad*, in sea-blue for the *Odyssey*. "Sing,
Goddess . . ." they began for the heroic tragedy,
but "Tell me, Muse . . ." for the heroic comedy
of manners.[1]

Tell me, Muse, of that ingenious man who travelled far
After he had overthrown the forts of Troy in war,
Visited many towns of men, and learnt their minds, while he
In his own heart suffered many griefs upon the sea
While he toiled to save himself and bring his comrades safely
    home.
Even so, he could not save his comrades. They were fools, and
    ate
The cattle of our Lord the Sun-God. Their own folly proved
    their fate.
Something of that story, Goddess, child of Zeus, to us relate.

Odysseus was the most "ingenious" man who
went to Troy. He won the war by his invention
of the Wooden Horse. And yet

When all the rest, as many as escaped sheer death at Troy,
Were at home, escaped from war and peril of the sea,
He alone, though longing for his wife and for his home,
Was kept by the bright nymph Calypso in her cave, for she

---

[1] *Odyssey*, i, 1–20.

95

Longed to have him as her husband, and she would not set him
    free.
But when amid the circling years at last the year was come
In which the gods had spun his thread of fate to travel home
To Ithaca (though even there he was not quite set free from care)
The gods began to pity him—except the Sea-God. He alone
Incessantly, implacably, was angry as before
Against the bright Odysseus till he reached his native shore.

How candid, yet how charitable, is the humour of
it! This man's genius won the war. He had that
passionate delighted interest in the minds of men
which is the master-key of genius. But he couldn't
manage to get home. And why? A bright-haired
nymph detained him. Surely Homer smiled. Is
not a contrast exquisitely hinted between the much-
enduring, spell-bound hero and the wife who holds
the fort for him at home against a host of suitors?
As for the Sea-God, he is still the same as ever.
Many an old campaigner from the Seven Seas
knows *him*. However, one fine day the Sea-God
was on holiday, and all the rest of the gods went
up to visit Zeus on Mount Olympus.

Fie! said Zeus, *These mortals! How they blame us gods and say*
All their troubles come from us. But it is also they,
By their own wicked folly get
Much grief beyond the portion set.[1]

That sounds convincing. Much virtue in that
"also." Had he said "It's *all* their own fault"—
well, we might have murmured, like that gentle
English lady who was heard to say in 1940, when
the minister gave out a hymn—"The fault is ours,
beneath thy rod we bow"—"I shall *not* sing that

[1] i, 32–34.

hymn, the fault is *not* mine. I'm not bowing under anybody's rod. I'm fighting."

The high gods understand. They only ask us to admit our folly does contribute something.

But this affair is Greek, so the debate goes on. To prove his point, the Father cites the case of an unmitigated scoundrel, Aegisthus, who, in spite of warning from the gods, seduced King Agamemnon's wife and murdered him on his return from Troy, and now has met the bad fate he so well deserved. Instantly there is a protest from the high god's daughter, that great lady who will some day give her name and something of her character to Athens. "Of course," Athena cries, "of course. So perish anyone who does the sort of thing that *he* did. But Odysseus! He's not wicked. He's not stupid. Why can't *he* get home?" "The weather, child, the Sea-God. That little trouble about Cyclops, you remember" . . . "However, since the Sea-God is on holiday, we might do something." "Thank you, Father. We'll send Hermes to Calypso presently. But first I'll fly to Ithaca and put some spirit into that young man, Odysseus' son."

The young man needs it. He is still a boy, and very young for his age. As Lawrence of Arabia, who wrote his wonderful translation in the racket of an R.A.F. canteen, observed—the boy's a prig. He is. Boys of some promise generally are. But think of this boy's history.

He was a baby when his father went to Troy,

some ten years old when the war ended. He is now about eighteen, and father hasn't come home. Everyone says he must be dead—Not mother! Years have passed, and everyone says she ought to marry. She says "no," or rather, "if," or "yes and no." For months and years, day after day, all day, the house has been infested by a gang of riotous, discourteous, self-invited guests, the suitors, whom his mother treats so very strangely. Why on earth can she not send them packing? Or make up her mind to face the facts and marry one of them? He hates it all. He cannot understand.

He doesn't realize—how should he?—what *she* knows only too well. If she yields, this boy will lose his birthright. If she sends them packing, they will certainly avenge the insult on her son. So she fights on for time, hoping against all hope for a miracle. She is "cattish, sly" says T. E. Lawrence. Yes, she fights like a wild cat, now fierce, now sleek and sly, for freedom and the boy. Perhaps the hardest thing to bear is this—he doesn't, mustn't understand!

One morning, when Telemachus sat, brooding and depressed, he saw a stranger at the threshold. Without a moment's hesitation, he rose with zealous hospitality and went to meet his guest: "Stranger, good cheer. You shall have friendly welcome here." This boy comes of good stock. He will do well.

It is, of course, Athena, in disguise. She talks to him, amid the hubbub. "What a strange state

98

of affairs! It must be very painful for you. Yes,
I know your father well. A fighter! And you need
him badly, don't you? If he were here. . . Oh,
certainly he'll come, if he's alive. If he's in chains,
he'll find a way. He'll manage. *Are* you his son?"
"My mother says so." "Ah—you won't be a
nameless nobody if you're *her* son."

That interview changes everything. He grows.
He walks among the suitors, unafraid, "a godlike
man." [1]

Meanwhile the minstrel sang and all sat silent and were still,
While he told his tale, how bitter by Athena's will
Was the Greek return from Troy. And in her upper room
The daughter of Icarios, discreet Penelope,
Heard and understood, and down the steep stair presently
Came, two serving-maidens with her, to the place
Where the suitors sat in Hall. There, covering her face
With a veil, that fairest among women, took her stand,
A serving-maid on either hand,
Close to the main pillar. There she wept awhile, then said:
Phemius, you know full well many tales that poets tell
For the fame and the delight of mortals. Tell them from your store
Any other tale than this, but of this tale no more:
It is too hard for me to bear. Indeed I am afflicted sore,
For there is one I long for always, and remember always, one
Known to fame throughout all Hellas, and in royal Argos known.
She spoke, and wise Telemachus made answer: *Mother, do not*
      chide
The trusty minstrel in your heart, because he sings for men's delight
Whatsoever tale he please, whatever way his heart indite.
It is not poets are to blame, but Zeus, who giveth mortal men,
Each and all, according to his pleasure, joy and pain.
Not Odysseus only, many others were denied
The joy of safe return from Troy, where many heroes died.
She heard, and marvelled when she heard, and to her chamber
      went,

---

[1] i, 206 ff. and 324.

Treasuring her son's wise word, and with her women wept
For her dear husband, till at last grey-eyed Athena sent
Gentle sleep to close her eyes, and peacefully she slept.[1]

We know the sequel—how the boy first made a brave, and therefore not quite useless, public protest, then went off in secret, on a voyage, to seek news of his father: how everywhere he heard more of his father's greatness, as a prince, a soldier, a shrewd counsellor and a good comrade, and how all the time the youth was growing stronger, more alive, more fit to help.

The suitors became nervous at his absence. They hatched a plot to kill him on the journey home. Penelope discovered. What was she to do? "Pray to Athena" said the Nurse. She prayed, and then, distracted, angry, desperately anxious, tossed in her bed—at her wits' end.

"Doubts and fears chased through her mind as they do through a lion's when he finds himself surrounded by the beaters and stands in terror as they stealthily close in." [2]

She is a hunted lioness. I quote this version of the noble simile with gratitude from Mr. E. V. Rieu's translation in the Penguin series.

At last she sleeps, and dreams her sister comes to her. It is Athena really. "Why are you distressed?"

First I lost my lion-hearted husband, who was excellent,
A prince among the Danaans, in every virtue eminent,
And now my well-belovéd son Telemachus is gone.[3]

---

[1] i, 328–364.　　　　[2] iv, 791 ff.　　　　[3] iv, 814 ff.

"Athena will take care of him. Do not be anxious." "But my husband? What of him?" "I cannot tell you that!" The vision fades.

So to Calypso's island. We are now to meet the hero, though we think we know him well already, through the eyes of those who love him and admire him and of some who hate but fear him. Homer dares to introduce him not as the majestic figure we perhaps expect, but as a lonely human waif, disconsolately gazing out to sea "as usual," "weeping because the nymph no longer pleased him."

Graciously, reluctantly, Calypso obeys orders. But she makes one last appeal. "Do you really so much want to go? Here you will never be cold or hungry, never grow old or die. And I think I am not less beautiful than she . . ." "Oh, far more beautiful. You are a goddess. But I want, I want to go."

The tools, the raft, the magic scarf which saves him, though at first he doesn't trust it—that's a poet's symbol of the little more past calculation which can save when the machines break down— the fight with the rough sea, and then the sleep under the heaped-up leaves in a thicket by the stream. "He was like the spark of fire a careful rustic covers with the ash at night so that the flame may be alive at morning." Then the waking, and Nausicaa.[1]

All night Odysseus lay there, fast asleep,

[1] v, 488-490, v, 85-109 and 115-121.

bruised, naked, helpless, close to death but still alive. At dawn a company of lovely maidens drove down in their mule-cart from the palace to the river-meadows to wash clothes, Princess Nausicaa and her friends.

So, when they reached the river, and the pools of water there,
Welling fresh to wash clothes clean however foul they were,
They loosed the mules from the waggon and hurried them away
To feed on the sweet clover by the eddying stream, while they
Fetched armfuls of the linen, filled the water-troughs, and then
Trampled the clothes beneath their feet, all working might and
    main
With such a zest to do their best in rivalry so keen
That very soon the work was done and every clout washed clean.
Then they spread the linen out in order on the strand
Where the shingle was kept cleanest by the waves that washed
    the land,
And bathed, and made their bodies bright with olive-oil, and ate
Their breakfast, while the hot sun dried the clothes. And after
    that
The princess and her serving maids together one and all
Threw off their bonnets from their heads and played a game of
    ball.

Their leader was white-armed Nausicaa, and she
Was beautiful, like Artemis the huntress, in the glades
Of high Taygetus or Erymanthus with her maids,
Hunting the boar or stag—the nymphs her playmates of the
    wild
Attending—all were fair to see, but none so beautiful as she
And Leto's heart is glad because her child,
With head held high, in majesty surpasseth all that company.
So chaste Nausicaa that day was seen
Among her maidens, manifestly Beauty's Queen.

Then Athena had another thought, one of her best.
Odysseus should awake and see Nausicaa.

The princess threw to a serving-maid, but the ball travelled wide
And fell in a deep eddying pool, whereat the maidens cried

Aloud, and bright Odysseus woke, and to his own heart said:
  Ah me!
Where am I now? What land is this? What kind of folk possess
This country? Proud and cruel men who know not righteousness?
Or friends to strangers, men of a god-fearing mind? I'll see.
I'll try the venture . . .

God-like? God-fearing? To me the word *theoeides*
looks ambiguous. Perhaps it comes to much the
same thing. Anyhow, the thought is Greek, and
I believe it came from the same source of inspiration as the Hebrew and the Christian word—"God
and my neighbour." These girls were Greek, as
Homer loved to think Greek girls could be. They
were mothers of the race which first taught
Greece, then, after a grim Roman interlude, the
rest of us to play our games for fun and friendship.
The Greeks called education "play" and study
"leisure" (*paideia*, *schole*), but they worked quite
hard as well. They had "good minds," as Homer
puts it.

When I read again the story of Odysseus in
Phaeacia I am reminded somehow of those first
two maxims of Confucius, which until lately every
boy and girl in China had to learn by heart: "To
learn, and always to be learning something, is it
not a pleasure?" "Is it not delightful to have
friends coming from afar?" The third good
maxim, "Never to strive for recognition of what
one does, is this not the trait of a gentleman?" I
fear, does not describe Alcinous, his guest Odysseus, or the Greeks of history. Or most of us?

At any rate, across the centuries, we owe to

Homer the delight of meeting friends like these
—the generous, absent-minded, vain, but altogether charming King Alcinous, his Queen and
undisputed governess, Arete, Nausicaa herself,
and those Phaeacian women whom Athena "taught
to make beautiful things—and she gave them
good minds as well";[1] the boys, too candid to be
tactful, too friendly to offend; the dancers and the
sailors; blind Demodocus, and, as their honoured
guest, Odysseus, now to be revealed in all his
subtlety of mind and energy of Spirit as he holds
them all entranced with story after story till the
sunset comes.

At last the twilight fell. He took his leave. The
good ship, laden with Phaeacian gifts, and lifting
as it ran, like a four-horse chariot, sped through
the darkness. On the deck Odysseus slept. He
had forgotten all his troubles. So they landed him
asleep, and when he woke he did not know he was
at home.

The truth is that Athena put a mist about the
island, partly for sheer fun, partly perhaps to test
him, partly to complete his education and increase
his faith. He needs it in his own way quite as
much as that boy needed it. Anyhow, just before
she sweeps the mist away, the goddess says: "I
cannot ever leave you, though you are unlucky,
because you have a gift of speech, quick wits and
a true heart."[2]

At the good swineherd's hut he met his son.

[1] vii, 110.   [2] xiii, 331 ff.

They planned and fought and won their fight together. Penelope still played her brave and subtle part, with just a touch of fresh bravado, even with a relish of excitement, but an aching sense that something wonderful,—she knew not what— might happen any moment. Then at the end, when Telemachus exclaimed on her because she seemed so slow to recognize her husband— "Mother, you are harder than a stone"—she answered:

Child, my heart is full of a great wonder. I can say
No word at all, nor question him at all. I cannot raise
My eyes to him that we might look each other in the face.
And yet if he has come, if it is true that he is home,
We shall recognize each other all the better, for we two
Have secrets he and I alone, and no one else may know.[1]

"It is beautiful," said Homer's wanderer Odysseus, in Phaeacia, "To listen to a poet, and to such a poet."

[1] xxii, 105–110 and ix, 3 f.

ATHENS, A GARDEN OF
THE MUSES

A CHORUS FROM EURIPIDES' *MEDEA*

AT night, alone in College rooms at Cambridge, Nathaniel Wedd, my tutor, had what he would have called "a *rum* experience," a dream or vision, from which there came to him, with thoughts of his own pupils, a new and deeper understanding of Euripides, his favourite Greek poet. While the memory was fresh he made a record, which was found among his papers when he died in September 1940, and was given me by his widow, the late Rachel Wedd, *née* White, of Newnham. Not quite all of it seems suitable for publication now, but I have ventured to include some extracts from it, since it was Wedd's thought which first suggested both the subject of this essay and much of what I hope has been worth saying in this book.

Enhupnion. Dream [Wedd wrote]. December 30, 1938. Tour round excavated Chetwynd Court, past the Club for Discussion etc., in room under my big room, and how it went on on different themes every time I passed until about 2 a.m., when it seemed to have stopped. How nice youths helped me about the slippery, muddy, runlet-wet ups and downs in the Chetwynd, round through the entrance, past the Lecture Club, into the front court and somehow up into rooms on the first floor, where young men, all known to me, discussed all sorts of things all night as a matter of course . . . I was treated quite naturally as one of themselves . . . There was much movement and life . . . I seem to have come and gone on the tours . . . After the last one the young men seem to have gone, and I thought, "Ah, they do go to bed then, ἄρα." The whole impression was delightful and exhilarating, and the affection of the young men warmed the air. On the last walk up the steep gully, I staggered and said, "This is not alcohol," and the youth who guided me by the arm said, "I'm not so sure of that," and then led me by the hand with a jolly warm pressure of friendliness and guided me so . . .

During these walks I thought from time to time, "I suppose I am a spirit moving among them in the spirit. Are they thus, and do they feel like this to me? They seem real, and they treat me as real, and I seem to get at their spirits in this way."

When Wedd wrote thus he was frail and nearly blind, but still in touch with pupils, writing to many, thinking of all with deep affection. He loved Cambridge and for more than fifty years helped others to revere her as a mother still crowned, in spite of wars and educational reformers, with many a gentle Muse and learned wit. In youth, we used to say, Wedd was a firebrand: certainly he never ceased to be a kindler of live sparks. He told us he had chosen Cambridge because he found the air of a certain famous Oxford College over-fragrant of "success," and King's, because another Cambridge College made an extra charge in Hall for pudding. Even at King's grave heads were sometimes shaken at his catholicity of taste in friends and books and language. When he heard a don say "bloody" was a word "used only by the lower classes," Wedd began to use the word himself. As Librarian of the Union, in the early eighties, he encouraged, nay incited undergraduates to ask for Zola. He devoured books for their spirit and their content, not as models of discretion or of style. He had learnt that from Abbott at the City of London School. Passionately he believed a University should be an Athens, not an Alexandria, and, like his friend the "Miners' Bishop" Westcott, he interpreted the Gospel in his own way as good news from Greece as well as Palestine. When he and Walter Headlam were rebuked for playing croquet on a Sunday, "I deplore," he said, "a faith so fragile that it trembles at the click of croquet-balls heard on the way to Chapel." That was Wedd. Of course he loved Euripides. Of course we loved him.

Well, he wrote of his dream-vision:

It was, I felt at the time, all wonderfully warm and exhilarating. In the room I talked with some of them about Euripides and then, either awake or again asleep, went off into a sketch of what Euripides is—the waist of the hour-glass which draws to itself the converging strands of ancient and modern wisdom, filters them and sends them out in divergent rays to light the world ever since. Chiefly he gave the stimulus to Socrates, his junior by fifteen years. He had a big library, and I imagined him as one of the circle described by Socrates in the *Memorabilia*, meeting, reading books, and discussing their problems together.

The passage to which Wedd referred is in Xenophon's *Memorabilia*, I. vi, 11:

When Antiphon said, "You are a just man, Socrates, but are not wise (*sophos*) to charge nothing for your teaching," Socrates replied, "Beauty and Wisdom are good or bad according to the way we use them. To sell beauty we call harlotry, but he who makes his friend a lover truly good and beautiful is *sophron*—temperate, safe-minded. Even so with *sophia*. I value friendship. That's the explanation. If I get anything good, I share it and try to teach whatever I think will help my friend to *arete*—

to excellence. Together we turn over the treasures left us written in their books by the wise men of old. If we find anything good, we note it, and we think it a great gain if in so doing we make friends with one another."

So Wedd imagined Socrates, a youth, like one of his own pupils, sitting with the older man and others, reading, arguing, listening, and making friends. Then he remembered how, in the *Alcestis*, produced in 438 B.C., when Socrates was about twenty-seven, Euripides forty-two and Aristophanes a child of eight, the Chorus sing [1] about old books and lore that teach us nothing but *Anagke*, and he noted the close parallel with Socrates' account of his own experience in the *Phaedo*.[2] Browning, I fancy, had the same thought. Here is his version, from *Balaustion*, of the Euripidean lines.

> They too, upborne by airy help of song
> And haply science that can find the stars,
> Had searched the heights, had sounded depths as well
> By catching much at books where logic lurked,
> Yet nowhere found they aught could overcome
> Necessity . . . nor any remedy
> To solace overburdened mortals, none.

If that reminds us of our own Victorian and post-Victorian zest for dusty answers wrung from narrow premises, the parallel with Socrates is closer still—his passion for "the Wisdom that they call the Science of Nature," his joy to hear that Anaxagoras thought Nous the cause of everything, his grief to learn what little use the man of science had for Nous, except to give the great machine a

[1] 961 ff. [2] 97B.

start, then leave it—yes, and leave *us* thinking, thinking that, since nobody *can* think without a brain or move without his limbs, the bones and sinews and grey matter are forsooth the cause of all we think and do and feel.

Finally Wedd recalled the praise of Athens in the *Medea* (421–445) as a place where happy people, moving in a bright pure air, are fed on Wisdom, and recognized, as M. Méridier has also done, in phrases like "the fair plant of the Muses, Harmony" and "Loves at work with Wisdom for the fostering of excellence" the promise of the *Phaedrus* and *Symposium*. Eros, he said, in Athens, and especially in the Socratic circle, meant something different from the normal Dorian Eros, which, in Sparta notably, promoted military courage and efficiency—though that too in the Theban Sacred Band was touched by the Pythagorean and Socratic influence; something different too from the good comradeship of athletes, praised by Aristophanes in his nostalgic picture of the good boy practising his running with a chaste companion at spring-time in the grand old days of Marathon. No, this was something new, peculiarly Athenian, this notion of a Love so linked with *Sophia* and *Arete* that *Philosophia* in Greek came to mean not "philosophy" in our sense, but "religion," and *sophos* meant "good, quite as much as learned anyway." Dr. Inge, Wedd thought, was wrong in saying that the Greeks lacked kindness for its own sake. "He is so pro-Greek," Wedd wrote,

"that he feels he must be 'fair' and say, anyway
the Christians brought in kindness." "Matthew
Arnold used to say that sort of thing about Israel
bringing in the thirst for righteousness, and had
to say that the Greeks lacked that pet virtue."

Really the Greeks lacked neither: the brotherhood of mankind,
the incompatibility of slavery with justice, the fatherhood of
God etc. and the unceasing desire to find out the laws that should
establish righteousness on earth—all this was Greek. The
difference between Stoic and Christian was the bias of the Greek
towards the intellectual, and of the Christian towards the moral
approach, basis or way of putting it. The one appeals to the
educated few, the other to the masses. What Jesus did was to
put by intuition or the instrument that supplements reason the
truths mediated by reason in philosophy. He put men in direct
touch with God or the Reality or . . . , and gave them the
certainty of immediate experience . . .

When Wedd wrote thus, as I have said, he was
frail and nearly blind, but he said, "if only I could
read, I would go through all Euripides to test it."
What I venture to ask readers of this essay is to
think again about this one play, the *Medea*, in the
light of Wedd's suggestion. Is it fact or fancy?
I for one believe it is a clue both to the purpose of
the play and to much else.

The *Medea* isn't by any means a pleasant play.
Certainly it's a play about unpleasant people—
Jason, a handsome, shrewdly calculating, unimaginative egoist, who thinks himself a model of
good-nature and good sense; Medea, fascinating,
utterly self-centred and malignant, the incarnation
of perverted passion, masquerading as romantic,

wounded love. From the Nurse's first words, "How I wish that good ship hadn't passed the straits—I wish that pine-tree hadn't ever been cut down—because my mistress wouldn't then have sailed with Jason to Iolkos—she was terribly in love with Jason—and she wouldn't have persuaded Pelias' daughters to destroy their father, and so *had* to move to Corinth," to Jason's cry in the last scene, "I was a fool to marry you, considering . . ." my sympathies go out to Pelias' daughters, to the murdered brother and the murdered children, not to Jason, nor emphatically to Medea—even if Paley says, "She is a woman of strong attachments . . . as a wife and mother not unamiable," and bids us, though she is "in some sense a wicked woman," to call her rather "a natural woman, who has not been taught" etc. I can't even feel, as Mr. Norwood does about Euripidean tragedies, "How terrible, and yet how like ourselves." No, when Medea kills her children she is far too sorry for herself to get my sympathy. The thing is ugly, ugly.

Why on earth, then, did Euripides produce the play? Partly, I suppose, because he liked a thriller. Many people do. Partly, no doubt, to give complacent, selfish prigs and morbid egoists a shock. But there is more than that to say. Against the ugliness Euripides has set in contrast his ideal for Athens of a happy people, moving in a bright pure air and fed on Wisdom. That is surely the clue.

Now for the play.

After the Prologue and the scene between the Nurse, the Paidagogos and the children, enter a group of ladies, sympathetic to Medea, just in time to hear her frantic cries within. Horrified, as well they may be, very sorry for her, they suggest—could Nurse induce her to come out and have a talk with them? It might help a little? Nurse is sceptical: "She's fierce, like a wild animal . . . fiercer than ever if you speak to her . . . well, well, I'll try." Nurse goes, and very nervously—oh, how they wish they could help—our ladies say or sing:

> Dullards, not wise, were our fathers, using the art
>> Of song that delights the ear,
> Only for banquets and festivals, scenes of good cheer;
>> None of them finding a way
> By the Muse, by the thrill of the voice and the harp, to allay
>> The pangs of the heart, whence come
> Death and the poison of hate for the doom of the home.[1]

They are good simple creatures, hardly fair to the Greek medical tradition which believed in psychotherapy by music long before Hippocrates; and hardly fair to the old poets. The Muses, Hesiod said, were born for "sweet forgetfulness of care and banishment of wrong." All the same, they say, old-fashioned poets are not *sophoi*, they are *skaioi*, clumsy, stupid. They don't use their art where it's most needed. They don't minister to minds diseased. They feel so helpless. How on earth are they to cope with their distracted friend.

I venture to suggest that this is the first state-

---

[1] *Medea*, 190–198.

ment of a theme we shall hear later, just suggesting
—only just suggesting here, just hinting—an
ideal Harmony which, though it heightens the
effect of the grim tale, does by the note of beauty
make it tolerable. That is in fact to be the function
of the Chorus, so that in contemplating Jason and
Medea we may know that Hell is murky, and yet,
ever and anon, catch, faint but unmistakable, the
music of the Magic Flute.

Medea comes. Her handling of the ladies is a
masterpiece of cunning—or of self-control, if anyone prefers that mitigating title. She isn't shouting now. No more screaming "Death to those
accurséd children and their father! May the whole
house crash in ruin!" Not a bit of it. She is all,
by turns, sweet reason, deference, apologetic
courtesy, indignant irony, heartbroken pathos.
Then, when she has the women in the hollow of
her hand, she tells them: "If I get my chance, I
mean to be revenged."

Oh yes, of course. We all approve. She has
won her first round. Enter Creon, whose decree
of banishment rouses our good ladies to such
a pitch of righteous indignation that, without
reserve, with fierce enthusiasm, they acclaim what
is in fact a monstrous plan. Medea means, and
says she means, if she can manage it, to murder
Jason and the King and the Princess. Assassina-
tion as a prelude to a glorious revolution! We
know the formula. Kind people who regard Medea
as the mouthpiece of the poet's liberalism, must

be shocked, one fears, by the consequences of such liberal propaganda. Our poor ladies are not shocked—not yet. She has caught them. They are swept away, bewitched, and break into a hymn of triumph for the brave new world. She has won the second round.

> Back in their courses shall the sacred rivers run.
> Changed shall be nature's order, her laws undone,
> And the customs of yore overthrown.[1]

And yet—and yet—will it be all so delightful? Of course it will, but we must have a different sort of poetry. Art must be *gleichgeschaltet*, truly democratic, yes, in a new sense, class-conscious. *Man* must be denounced! Alas, they naïvely complain, Apollo hasn't given women in full measure the essential gift of song. If they had it, what a story . . .!

It's all the man's fault, Jason's fault, of course. And yet it's natural to shed pious tears about the prospect. Decent human feeling (*aidos*) and the graciousness that waits on loyalty to covenants (*horkon charis*) have fled from earth to heaven, like Hesiod's Nemesis and Aidos, veiling their faces and abandoning the sinners of this iron age.[2]

That's double-edged in such a context. Enter Jason.

To confirm our dark forebodings, we and the ladies have to witness such a scene of utterly self-centred mutual recrimination that it would be difficult to say which of the precious pair is the

[1] 410 ff.   [2] 439 f.

more hateful, Jason, the sophist of prosaic, worldly common sense, or she, the sophist of romance.

Anyhow, on our ladies, the effect is a kind of fluttering distress:

> From loves that keep no measure, none hath seen
> Fruit of good fame or virtue; yet Love's Queen
> Hath grace beyond all other powers to bless
> Hearts that she visiteth in gentleness
> With love, but no excess.
> Grant, O dread Queen, that I may never know
> The hurt none cures, the all-consuming fire,
> The poison of the arrows of desire,
> Shot from the golden bow.
> Grant me true heart's content, with modesty
> Of mind, heaven's fairest gift, Sophrosyne . . . [1]

"Make innocence my friend," as Mr. Gilbert Murray puts it, summing up the matter in another admirable phrase, "O Cyprian, sift, Keen-eyed, for me love's good and evil gift."

These are far better thoughts of love than Jason and Medea have or ever have had. They make us think of a much better place than rich, licentious, scheming Corinth. Enter Aegeus, King of Athens.

Quite a good fellow, this, we feel at once. Not clever, not romantic. Just a good Athenian, worried about his childlessness, perplexed by an ambiguous oracle, simple-hearted, glad to help when he finds Medea in distress. As a good Athenian should, he promises the poor unfortunate a refuge, nay, a home in Athens. She offers in return, and he, in his simplicity, accepts, the promise of a cure for the misfortune that has kept

[1] 628–636.

him childless. He little knows—we know: Euripides has already dramatized the incident [1]—this is the way she means to keep her promise. This devil—yes, she is a devil—will incite the good old man, her benefactor, to destroy his only son, as yet unborn, and long to be unrecognized, the hero Theseus. In the nick of time, as it happens, her plot will be exposed and the prince saved. But that's another story.

She promises and he believes her. She binds him with an oath. Puzzled, but unsuspicious still, he goes his way.

Then—then—the moment he is gone, she turns in ghastly triumph to the Chorus and announces that she means to kill her children. So much for the promise of the brave new world! At that point these simple-minded women yearn for Athens, unpolluted, wise and kind: [2]

> Erechtheus' children are from ancient days
> A happy race,
> Born of blest gods, sons of a holy land
> Smirch'd by no spoiler's hand.
> There, exquisitely moving in a bright pure air, they feed
> On Wisdom. There, 'tis said,
> By the Pierian Choir, the virginal nine Muses long ago
> Golden-haired Harmony was planted and did grow.
>
> Love's Queen herself, that ancient story says,
> Over that place,
> Dipping her pitcher in Kephissus' fair
> Fresh waters, wafts an air

---

[1] In a play now lost, the *Aegeus*. Euripides was clearly fascinated by Medea's criminal career. One of his earliest plays (455 B.C.) was *The Daughters of Pelias*.
[2] *Medea*, 824–850.

Of gentleness. She twines a fragrant braid
Of roses for her head,
Then sends her Loves to share the throne of Wisdom—only so,
When the Loves work with Wisdom, all fair fruits of Virtue
    grow.

How can the city where those sacred waters flow
Endure thy presence, blood-polluted and unblest?
How can a land where friends and lovers freely come and go
Welcome the murderess of her children with the rest?

How indeed? These women, fascinated by Medea,
blinded by their pity—she is very beautiful and
very clever and it's not for nothing that she is the
grandchild of the sun-god—draw the line at that.
Kill your own children! Suddenly they see, and
they implore her to relent.

Polymathia, as Heraclitus said, does not teach
understanding (*nous*). Astonishing how learned
men can miss the mark. Nauck scoffed at the idea
of Wisdom "growing wild" and the Athenians
"browsing on it" like a herd of cattle. Wecklein
substituted *phorban*—food or fodder—for *sophian*
—more *praktisch*, more substantial! Even great
Verrall told us, *sophia* meant "roughly" at that
time in Athens "culture" and *arete* meant here
"artistic excellence" and had not the later "ethical
meaning." Wilamowitz gave his vote for *Wissenschaft*—"*erhabener Wissenschaft geistiger Brot*"—
and told us of a string of German Loves, *Kunst*,
Anmut, *Streben*, *Sehnen*, which collaborate with
Wissenschaft for the achievement of what I can only
call a doctorate—*da lernt das Höchste zu leisten der
Mensch*. Deutschland is great, a German scholar

118

said in 1914, because she has *Fleiss*, *Arbeit*, *Leistungsfähigkeit*. "Yes, of course," said Maynard Keynes, "but *WAS zu leisten?*"

Even to Mr. Page and Mr. Higham, *sophia* means "Art," or rather, as Mr. Page in his commentary tells us, "knowledge generally, but especially in arts and sciences"—*erhabener Wissenschaft* again,—while *erotes* are "the spirits of devotion," but "especially devotion to the arts," and *arete*, *pantoia arete*, "as usual," means "goodness in something, more especially skill in the arts," *not* "goodness in the moral sense."

"Oh dear, oh dear," these ladies are supposed to say, "In Athens, with her good connections, her perfect climate, her exquisite way of walking, her devotion to the arts and excellence in all of them, you'll not be welcome. No young lady who has cut her brother into pieces—you were terribly in love, of course, with Jason—and has settled in Iolkos and persuaded those poor dears to cut their father up and boil him—well, he was a wicked uncle: that was some excuse—but really, if you murder your own children, no, you'll not be welcome there. Wait a few centuries. O God, O Montreal! Shades of Nero and the Borgias!"

Surely to talk of *sophia* here as "culture" or as "knowledge," of *erotes* as "devotion to the arts and sciences," and of *pantoia arete* as "skill in all of them," is nonsense, precious nonsense, even if it comes from scholars to whose work upon this play we owe a debt of gratitude for much that helps.

I venture to submit that what the ladies say and mean is something simpler, something more like this: "Don't do it, dear. If you do, you won't be good enough for Athens. Don't do it. Athens is too good to tolerate that sort of thing."

Elsewhere, I am delighted to observe that Mr. Page relents. After his gallant skirmish against those of us who think that anybody before Plato had the least idea that *arete* had anything to do with humdrum Anglo-Saxon virtue, he goes on to say, "Love works with Wisdom" in this wise:

> The passion . . . commonly limited to physical love between men and women is here diverted to other creatures of beauty, sublimated by being applied to poetry, music and philosophy.

That is excellent, so far as it goes. But why not add, "especially and obviously, in this context, to the art of making life worth living in the home and the community by common human decencies, including the domestic virtues?"

When the Muses at the marriage of Harmonia sang "What's beautiful is dear," what did they mean? I do not doubt that, being Greeks and ladies, they thought of dancing and deportment, as well as poetry and music; and possibly, nay probably, they thought, though not perhaps with quite the same enthusiasm, of "the arts in general": and nobody—not any Greek at any rate—is likely to suppose that they excluded mathematics, or anything whatever that is really fine. But certainly, quite certainly, they did include what everybody wishes for a bride and bridegroom, health, good

looks, a nice house and good children, and what
are even more essential, loving-kindness, mutual
forbearance and good sense. All these things the
Greeks thought good and beautiful, and so they are.

All very well. We are talking about Athens,
Periclean Athens. What about women? What
about love and marriage then and there?

Three years ago, in New York, at the Metro-
politan Museum, I had the happiness of talking
with Miss Richter, who showed me a delightful
Attic *hudria* depicting Eros with a maiden, and
told me about others. Their comparatively early
date, fourth century at latest, rules out the notion
that these lovers represent Eros with Psyche,
though the type points forward to the myth which
symbolizes the Platonic doctrine of the soul
immortalized by love. Miss Richter thinks these
charming vases were not funerary urns—at any rate
not only that—but treasured household vessels,
suitable and very likely often used as presents to a
bride. Certainly their spirit and the gentleness of
Eros with the maiden suggest that, though through
Socrates and Plato Eros did become the type of
love between good comrades in the search for
truth—the marriage of true minds—Eros was also,
at his best, a type of love between a girl and boy,
a husband and a wife.

Tell me, Muse, said Homer, and she told him
how Odysseus learnt the minds of men and came
to this conclusion, among others: "There is nothing better than when wife and husband are of one

mind in the home."[1] Euripides meant us to
remember that. He makes the Nurse misquote
and misapply it—not without irony as well as
pathos—in the first lines of the play. And the
word that Homer used, *homophroneonte*, of the
good wife and husband, was the word which
Hesiod used, *homophrones*, when he said about the
Muses, "Well do they agree." Do scholars really
think that when Penelope sighed,

> First I lost my lion-hearted husband, who was excellent,
> A prince among the Danaans, in every virtue eminent,

pantoiais aretaisi meant to her, because she lived
in old-world, pagan Ithaca, only that he was good
in battle and in council and in carpentry—not
good in any modern "moral" sense, not good to
have at home? I don't.

"What sort of people . . .?" asked Odysseus.
"Savage, arrogant, unfair? Or friends to strangers,
men of a god-fearing, godlike Mind?" That is
sophia in germ. We are still a long way from the
thought of Anaxagoras the friend of Pericles and
of Euripides; and further still from what some
added—Euripides himself in certain moods, and,
of course, Socrates, "If *nous* is the first cause,
perhaps Man's Mind, the greatest miracle, has as
its origin and destiny a spark divine." But what of
Pindar's Sophia?[2] "Sing oracles, O Muse. I will
interpret." "By reason of the *sophia* of Leto's son,
the eagle sleeps, and the fierce war-god lays aside

---

[1] *Od.* vi, 182 ff. *Theogony*, 60.
[2] Pindar, *Fr.* 150 (Bergk), *Pyth.* i, 12–26, *Pyth.* vi.

his spear, but evil spirits whom Zeus loves not shrink in terror from the music." Pindar's *sophia*, as he is never tired of telling us, is something better than a *techne*, and it's not by any means indifferent to moral excellence. "Dear boy, you've won your race and very properly proclaimed your father victor. Like Antilochus, if need be, you would willingly, I am sure, lay down your life for him." That is Pindar's *sophia*. It is inspired by Eros. It is meant to foster *arete*. The conception of Love throned with Wisdom for the fostering of Virtue is, in fact, the fruit of a tradition which such men as Pericles and Sophocles, Euripides and Aristophanes inherited and reinterpreted in many ways, and tried to share, each in his own way, not with a small exclusive aristocracy, but with all Athens, and so, ultimately, with us all.

The word *Harmonia* suggests another strain not less important. The thought that the nine Muses, born of Memory and of the Wisdom of the Counsellor "a little way below the highest height," do well agree and have the Graces for their neighbours and Love lodging near, once it has passed through the Ionian and Pythagorean schools of thought and intuition, could become—and here I am delighted to acknowledge Mr. Page's beautiful and lucid exegesis—something like this: "The Muses, different, yet at one, create an essence not themselves . . ." and "since Harmony inevitably is associated with her mother Aphrodite we are led to the conception of Excellence as the harmony of the passions and the understanding." That is well said, well imagined, true. It is an echo, is it not, of what Pythagoras, the greatest of the early Greek philosophers, divined?

Hell is murky, but the Magic Flute plays on. Wedd saw his vision on the eve of 1939. He knew the challenge that was coming to our Athens. Euripides produced this play in the spring of 431 B.C., when war had just begun. Surely his praise of Athens as a place where Aphrodite, drawing water from Kephissus, sends her Loves to work with Wisdom, was a prayer and not a boast. A few months later Pericles stood in the Cerameicus, exhorting the Athenians to gaze upon their city's greatness and become her lovers. When he told them, "We love Wisdom, but it doesn't sap our manhood; we love beauty, but it doesn't make us precious and extravagant," his thought, his prayer for Athens was essentially the same. So was the thought of Sophocles when he composed his Testament of Beauty, *Oedipus at Colonus*, a little while before he died and Athens fell:

> Here gleams the golden crocus. Here are springs
> That never fail, nor leave their wanderings
> Till from pure founts, Kephissus in full flood,
> Laving Earth's breast, gives life. Nor is this wood
> Shunned by the Muses. Nay, the Queen of Love
> Herself with golden chariot-rein doth haunt this wood.[1]

It is an echo of our Ode from the *Medea*, and, after all the wrong and tumult of the war, the prayer is still the same.

[1] *O.C.* 684 ff.

Was it answered? Yes, I think, and no. The cruel schoolmaster who makes his pupils coarse and cruel like himself had great success. He always has. Towards the end Athens almost, not quite, deserved to be defeated. She fell, and the restored "democracy" killed Socrates. And yet, thanks to her poets and to Pericles—for Plato was unjust to him—and thanks especially to Socrates, her greatest lover, though he was in life rejected, Athens, the Athens of the spirit, lived. For many centuries her garden walks, especially the groves of the Academy, were thronged by young and old in search of Wisdom and the company of friends. Nor did the stream of inspiration from Kephissus quite run dry, even when priests and pedants of Byzantium secured the closing of the Schools. The poet's fancy of Love throned with Wisdom, reillumined by the life and martyrdom of Socrates, and reinterpreted by Plato, was linked with his analysis of the four fundamental virtues, Courage, Temperance, Justice, Wisdom, and became a symbol of the grace by which a soul that loves and practises those virtues may rise to a more perfect wisdom and, so far as mortals may, see God.

A thousand years after Euripides composed his Ode, a Christian lawyer and imperial administrator, Marianus, wrote this epigram "On a Statue of Love, wearing a garland and carrying three others." [1]

[1] *Plan. Anth.* Appendix, 201, Mackail, xii, 45.

125

"Where is your straining bow, and where the darts
You shot, to pierce, fast fixed, through mortal hearts?
Where are your wings? Your cruel torch? Why bear
Three garlands in your hand, although you wear
One on your head?" Because I trace my birth
Not to the common Cyprian, nor to Earth.
Because the raptures that I promise spring
From joy in no such base material thing.
In men's pure Minds I light the flame of thought,
Whereby through learning souls to heaven are brought.
Of Virtue's Crowns, three in my hand I bear,
But Wisdom's Crown, the best, is what I wear.

Was that, as Mackail suggested, Marianus'
answer to another poet who made Love a country
lad?[1]

Call me not him of Lebanon. Not for me
Love-talk of youth by night and revelry.
Son of a neighbour Nymph, a country lad am I
Who simply dig my garden. That is why
I wear four crowns. Four seasons crown my head,
By this dear fruitful orchard garlanded.

If so, I think the country lad has won. He is not
smug, like Marianus. Was he thinking of the
Canticles?—"come with me from Lebanon, my
spouse," and how the Syrian goddess, once Pande-
mos, had yielded to the rightful Queen of Heaven?
Anyhow, *il faut cultiver son jardin*, and for us it is
to the purpose to remember that, when Dante rose
from the dead air of the Inferno to the more
delectable clime where souls are purified, he saw
first, "making the whole East laugh," the planet
Venus who gives strength to Love, and then four
stars, in which all heaven rejoiced, the stars of the

[1] *Plan. Anth.* Appendix, 201, Mackail, xii, 202.

four virtues. How eagerly then he listened to the
spirit of the friend who sang for him his own old
philosophic love-song: *Amor che nella mente mi
ragiona.* We think again how, in the Earthly
Paradise, after the invocation of the Springs of
Helicon and of the Muses, and the pageant of the
Elders, crowned with *fleurs de luce* and singing
"Blest for ever be thy beauties," and the four
beasts, garlanded with the green leaves of Hope,
he saw, beyond the mystic car three ladies robed
in white and emerald and red, Faith, Hope and
Charity, these three, and after them four ladies,
clad in purple. Who were they? Their leader,
Wisdom, had three eyes, to see past, present,
future. It was the gift the Muses brought to
Hesiod on Helicon.

When the procession ends, with the beloved
physician, Luke, and Paul, the bearer of the
sword, and four of humble aspect—Peter, James,
Jude and John, all turn towards the Car as to their
peace, and one sings *"Veni, Sposa di Libano"*
thrice, and all the rest sing "Hallelujah," as the
saints at the last trump shall sing with reclad
voices. Then, while a hundred ministers and
messengers of Life sing *Benedictus* . . . strewing
flowers above, around . . . *manibus o date lilia* . . .
Beatrice at last appears in garments flame-coloured
and green and white. And on her head she wears
Athena's crown of olive. Why? Because *philosophia* to Dante is still *uso amoroso di Sapienza.*

Soon as the lofty Virtue which already pierced me ere I passed

127

from boyhood smote upon my sight, I turned with the same
trust with which a little child runs to his mother, when he is
afraid or troubled, and said to Virgil—"Less than a drachm of
blood is there in me that trembles not. *Conosco i segni dell'
antico amore.*"

Strange, do you think, at such a moment to
quote Dido's word to Anna, spoken just when the
unruly passion took possession of her, challenging
the old true love? That too was Dante's story, and,
when Beatrice tenderly rebukes and yet consoles
him, he is like a child whose mother "pities him
and therefore must reprove him."

Hell is murky, but the Magic Flute plays on.
In our own generation we have learnt again the
truth of Shelley's prophecy, which is an echo from
our Chorus. After the vision which the Fury
shows Prometheus of the young Christ crucified
and of the cruelty inflicted in His name on man
by man, he speaks of something worse, unseen,
unheard:

> Terror survives
> The ravin it has gorged . . . The loftiest fear
> All that they would disdain to think were true . . .
> They dare not devise good . . .
> The Wise want Love, and those who love want Wisdom,
> And all best things are thus confused to ill.

And again, in the vision at the end, when conquest
is led captive, the same Euripidean thought is
dominant:

> Love from its awful throne of patient power
> In the *wise* heart from the last giddy hour
> Of dread endurance . . . springs
> And folds over the world its healing wings.

MUSIC AT BELMONT

WE heard the sentence and the pardon. We heard Shylock say, "I am content," and then, "I am not well. Send the deed after me." The Court rose, the Duke courteously entreated the young advocate to dinner, graciously accepted his excuse,

> I humbly do desire your grace of pardon,

then with his magnificoes withdrew. The curtain of the tiring-house was closed.

Below, at the Clerk's table, Nerissa still sat, busily engrossing Shylock's deed, but glancing every now and then with mischief in her eyes at Gratiano. Meanwhile Bassanio offered Portia the three thousand ducats, and his friend Antonio, with deeper understanding, offered "love and service evermore." "Take some remembrance," pleads Bassanio, learning better manners, "as a tribute, not a fee."

> Grant me two things, I pray you,
> Not to deny me, and to pardon me.

Portia is radiant. He has begged her pardon. Then, with a flash of inspiration, turning to Antonio, "give me your gloves," she says, "I'll wear them for your sake," and to her husband,

And for your love I'll take this ring from you.
Do not draw back your hand. I'll take no more,
And you in love shall not deny me this.

Bassanio denies her now, and for the best of
reasons. Glad at heart, she murmurs, "Peace be
with you," and so takes her leave.

So swiftly, and so beautifully has the poet
"posted to oblivion," in Granville Barker's phrase,
the tragic tension, and announced the theme of the
delightful sequel—"Love and service . . . pardon
. . for your love . . . and you in love shall not,
deny me . . . pardon . . . Peace be with you."

Portia withdraws. Nerissa follows. While they
are still in sight, crossing the great Elizabethan
stage, Antonio advises. "Let him have the ring
. . . for his deservings and my love." Bassanio
assents, and Gratiano runs to overtake them with
the gift. Portia accepts "most thankfully," then,
with an air of innocence, "I pray you, show my
youth old Shylock's house." Two whispered
sentences assure us that Nerissa needs no prompt-
ing. She too will have her ring, and she will play
her part in the outfacing and outswearing with the
best. All go their ways. The stage is empty for a
moment. Then the traverse curtain draws, dis-
closing, I suppose, a chamber, dimly lit by candles.
whence servants come, a few with torches and the
rest with greenery and rushes, which they strew,
and so transform the judgment-hall to a fair
garden, and the lawyers' table to a grassy mound
—just as to our delight at Harrow Shakespeare's

inspired producer, Mr. Ronald Watkins, made of
Quince's bench a flowery bank and of the work-
shop an enchanted wood.[1]

The servants take their torches out with them.
They are not needed. All withdraw, and for a
moment there is silence. Then from the house
come Jessica and Lorenzo, both deep in love, both
nimble-witted, one a man who knows, or thinks
he knows, the world's ways, one a quick impulsive
girl. Their talk, we guess, will be an equal match
of thrust and parry, and will end with laughter and
a kiss of peace.

Lorenzo speaks, and lo! the miracle has happened. We are in the moonlit avenue of Belmont,
Portia's home.

> The moon shines bright. In such a night as this,
> When the sweet wind did gently kiss the trees
> And they did make no noise, in such a night
> Troilus methinks mounted the Trojan walls
> And sighed his soul towards the Grecian tents
> Where Cressid lay that night.

Jessica understands. There is a hint, in that—
no more, but a lover's hint for her of a man's truth,
a woman's frailty. So she counters with the name
of her who won from Cressid's poet—"God forbid
but that a woman can Be as true and loving as a
man," Thisbe's true faith was just as much a pro-
verb in those days as Cressid's weakness. So

[1] For an account of this transformation see pp. 22–28 of Mr.
Ronald Watkins's essay, *Moonlight at the Globe* (Michael Joseph),
1946.

> In such a night
> Did Thisbe fearfully o'ertrip the dew
> And saw the lion's shadow ere himself,
> And ran dismay'd away.

She suits the action to the word, I think, and runs a little way, then turns inviting his pursuit. He teases her, holds back, as if, forsooth, like great Aeneas, he could ever leave her stranded.

> In such a night
> Stood Dido with a willow in her hand
> Upon the wild sea-banks, and waved her love
> To come again to Carthage.

I like to think that at that moment Thisbe-Jessica is standing on the rush-strewn bank, incarnate mischief, just out of reach, a little out of breath, and flashes back at him,

> In such a night
> Medea gathered the enchanted herbs
> That did renew old Aeson.

Jason's father! Fie, Jessica. That's too much to the point, a palpable hit for someone. Medea helped her man to win the Golden Fleece. And so, Lorenzo? Most lovingly, but with a spice of mischief, comes the riposte:

> In such a night
> Did Jessica steal from the wealthy Jew
> And with an unthrift love did run from Venice
> As far as Belmont.

The wheel has come full circle, and it is her turn to say:

> In such a night
> Did young Lorenzo swear he loved her well,
> Stealing her soul with many vows of faith
> And ne'er a true one.

What can he say to that?

> In such a night
> Did pretty Jessica, like a little shrew,
> Slander her love, and he—forgave it her.

With that, I think she runs to him. She is a child who loves and trusts him. He takes her in his arms.

Was it an accident that "wealthy Jew" chimed, as we heard the words, with "little shrew"? Shakespeare knew what he was doing when he made Lorenzo say she "stole" from Shylock. She did— some jewels and some ducats for her dowry. But Shakespeare understood much better than some Cambridge editors and wasn't shocked a bit. She forfeited, or thought she did, a fortune when, with an unthrift love, she ran to Belmont. What would have happened had she stayed? Shut in the home which was to her "a hell," denied society of friends, forbidden to look out of window or attend to music, and condemned to listen to the talk of Tubal, Chur and Shylock about ducats, hate, revenge, and "twenty times the value of the sum, Antonio's flesh," she must have grown a shrew indeed, and worse. She stole some jewels and some ducats, but Lorenzo, when he stole her soul by vows of faith, stole it from Shylock, not from her, rescued it from the hell that was called home, and gave her liberty to grow in grace and stature. She has wit and she loves music, and she loves Lorenzo. She will be a mother and a wife. In the sweet air of Belmont, her young spirit flowers. That is the

133

poet's thought, and that is why already he has made her say she likes the lady of the house "past all expressing," adding, rather wistfully, that

> It is very meet
> The Lord Bassanio live an upright life,
> For, having such a blessing in his lady,
> He finds the joys of heaven here on earth.

"And he—forgave it her." This happy dialogue in which two lovers dally with the innocence of love "as in the old age," capping one another's verses like Sicilian shepherds, but more courtly, is of course a prelude to the business of the ring, its fun, its happy ending. But it is a preparation also for a movement in a nobler strain, which heralds Portia's coming.

When Chaucer's Troilus had taken leave of Cressid, he lived "as one who stood betwixen hope and dread," and made a song, which he would sing with a soft voice and sighs, when nobody was near,

> O Star of which I lost have all the light . . . ,

and night by night, he stood "the bright moon to behold," and "all his sorrow told." "Upon the walls fast eke would he walk, And to himself would talk."

> Lo, yonder is mine owne lady free,
> Or else yonder, there the tentes be,
> And thence cometh this air that is so soote
> That in my Soul I feel it doth me boote.

The "sweet air" came, he fancied, from his lady's sighs, because, it seemed to him, no breeze stirred anywhere in Troy except upon the walls just where he stood.

Shakespeare remembered that, and he remembered too how, when the lover learnt the truth, and fought and died, his "light ghost blissfully" rose to the seventh sphere,

> And there he saw with full avisement
> The erratic Stars, harkening Harmonie
> With sounes full of Heaven's Melodie.

Thence, looking down, he saw this little world, with all its vanities, "this world that passeth soon as floures fair," and in himself he laughed and went his way to the place Mercury appointed.

All this the poet had in mind when he composed these last scenes of his comedy. From the first mention of the moon, the sweet wind, and the soul, to Portia's final "Pardon me, Bassanio," the whole is a dramatic lyric, spoken music, reminiscent of the pastoral and Chaucer, classical in form, but fresh in every detail, exquisitely happy.

"I would outnight you," Jessica declares, "did nobody come." Somebody does come, and enchantment is suspended for a moment, but the spell not broken. It is what corresponds in music to a passage of transition.

Two messengers bring great news. First Stephano:

> My mistress will before the break of day
> Be here at Belmont . . .

But she "strays about," he says, at holy crosses,

where "she kneels and prays for happy wedlock hours." Stephano, of course, was eager to press on. She "strayed about." "Who comes with her?" Lorenzo asks?

> None but a holy hermit and her maid.

Why, in the name of commonsense, asked Dr. Johnson, this holy, quite unnecessary hermit?

Because, I venture to suggest, she does pray anxiously. She knows Bassanio. She loves and understands him, and she knows how much depends on her. This mention of her prayers, and when she comes, the presence of the hermit, silent though he is, can teach us something of her quality. Hers is a spirit, passionate in love, but governed always by a fine intelligence, and never, even in the frolic of outfacing and outswearing, out of tune.

In other words, this quiet undertone sustains for us the music of the prelude—"they did make no noise . . . soul . . . soul . . . and he forgave it her."

Launcelot's jolly "Sola! Wo, Ha, Ho! . . . a post come from my Master," is a different matter, and by contrast heightens the effect of the return to the main theme—"Sweet soul, let's in . . . and yet . . . Why . . . Bring your music forth into the Air."

> How sweet the moonlight sleeps upon this bank.
> Here we will sit, and let the sound of Music
> Creep in our ears. Soft stillness and the night
> Become the touches of sweet Harmony.

136

As familiar, I suppose, as any lines of Shakespeare, and as comfortable to the English ear. No single note of Latin: two Greek words, Music and Harmony: the rest just English. As for the repetition of what Mr. Rylands has called "Shakespeare's darling word," "sweet moonlight ... music ... and sweet harmony," it marks the period and makes of the four lines a lyric stanza.

Shakespeare had certainly less Greek than Latin, but we can say, thanks to Professor Baldwin's masterly analysis both of the plays and of the normal Grammar School curriculum in Shakespeare's time, that Stratford gave him what a boy to-day, who has imagination, will be lucky if he gets. He started reading, imitating and discussing Latin verses very early with old Mantuan (whom I suspect he found a bore), and then with Virgil's *Eclogues*, Ovid, especially *Metamorphoses* for the stories, and then parts of the *Aeneid*, happily the best, Books 1 and 2 and 4 and 6. All these he knew and loved and never could forget.

But Greek? Not much more probably than a few anecdotes and "sentences" (proverbial maxims and the like) and a few verses of the Gospels. But would it not be strange if such a poet, many of whose friends were scholars, having fallen, as he did, in love with Ovid and the Latin pastoral, never for curiosity glanced at Theocritus, or asked a friend to help him with a construe of a few lines, just to show him why this poet was so much beloved? Did he? Who knows? Not I. But this is certain. Anyone to-day who knows even a very little Greek and looks at the first *Idyll* of Theocritus (in Greek, but with a "crib"), will hear from the first lines on the first page this music:

Sweet is the whispering of yonder pine that maketh melody over the waterspring, and sweet your piping, goatherd: after Pan you'll take the second prize.

Shepherd, your song is sweeter than the waterfall that gushes down among the rocks . . .

Come, goatherd, sit upon this shelving bank, and pipe for me . . .

No piping now. It is high noon, when Pan's asleep. It's dangerous to wake him.

Very well, then. Sing your song of Daphnis and I'll give you *such* a prize.

Was there any English version published soon enough for Shakespeare, if he happened on it, to have read it? I am not scholar enough to know. There is no version of this poem, the first *Idyll*, in the selection published by the University of Oxford in 1588 and dedicated to E.D.—perhaps Sir Edward Dyer, author of "My Mind to me a Kingdom is." And as for the poems there translated, such lines as these convey no more than a faint echo—hardly even that—of the Greek music:

Ye pleasant springs and plants, would Daphnis had
As sweet a voice as have the nightingales . . .
Sweet is the cow-calf's voice and sweet her breath doth smell . . .
'Tis sweet in summer by a spring abroad to dwell . . .

And, from a goatherd, this:

O Daphnis, what a dulcet mouth and voice thou hast!
'Tis sweeter thee to hear than honeycomb to taste.

Still less can we suppose that Latin versions, such

138

as that of Helius Eobanus (Hagenau, 1530),
Winsheim (Frankfurt, 1558) or Andreas Divus
(Basel, 1554) much helped.

> dulcem susurrum et pinus, caprarie, illa
> quae apud fontem canit, dulce autem et tu
> fistula canis . . . ,

for example.

But what matter? Pastoral was in the air, and
Shakespeare's magic is his own.

> Sit, Jessica: look how the floor of heaven
> Is thick inlaid with patines of bright gold.
> There's not the smallest orb which thou behold'st
> But in his motion like an angel sings,
> Still quiring to the young-eyed Cherubins;
> Such Harmony is in immortal Souls;
> But whilst this muddy vesture of decay
> Doth grossly close it in, we cannot hear it.
> *[Enter Musicians.*
> *Jessica.* I am never merry when I hear sweet music.
> *Lorenzo.* The reason is, your Spirits are attentive:
> Come, ho! and wake Diana with a hymn.
> With sweetest touches pierce your Mistress' ear,
> And draw her home with music.

Here is Latin, and in plenty—patines, orb and
motion: vesture and immortal and attentive spirits:
but still Greek. Music, sweet Harmony, angel,
quiring, hymn, sweet Music—all are Greek. The
Cherubins are Hebrew. Notice too the lovely
sequence—The moon sleeps . . . wake Diana with
a hymn.

The moment passes and Lorenzo talks, while
Jessica sits silent. Very well he talks, like a kind
husband—I had almost said, a kind Victorian
husband, but the race is not extinct. It is in effect

a little sermon that he preaches about Orpheus and the power of music and its limitations, with the moral pointed at "the man who has no music in himself, Nor is not moved by concord of sweet sounds."

> Let no such man be trusted. Mark the music.

One suspects that Jessica's attention may have wandered for a moment?

Portia's quiet entry does not break the spell. She is too far off at first to hear the music, but she sees the lights of home:

> How far that little candle throws its beams.
> So shines a good deed in a naughty world.

To Nerissa's comment, "When the moon shone we did not see the candle," she replies:

> So doth the greater glory dim the less:
> A substitute shines brightly as a King
> Until a King be by . . .

She is thinking of Bassanio, and at that moment hears the music:

> Music! Hark! . . .
> Methinks it is much sweeter than by day.

Do we not remember how, when her Bassanio was just about to choose, she said, "Let music sound . . ."?

> Then, if he lose, he makes a swan-like end,
> Fading in music. . . . He may win,
> And what is music then? then music is
> Even as the flourish when true subjects bow
> To a new-crowned monarch.

"Silence bestows that virtue," sagely says Nerissa, but her mistress, because joy is in her heart, breaks into a gay catalogue of birds, crows, larks and nightingales, the goose, the wren, and bids the music cease:

> Peace, ho! The moon sleeps with Endymion
> And would not be awaked.

Lorenzo.   That is the voice
> Or I am much deceived, of Portia.

Portia.   He knows me as the blind man knows the cuckoo,
> By the bad voice.

Lorenzo.   Dear lady, welcome home.

Portia's first words to Lorenzo are, "We have been praying for our husbands' welfare." It is true. Bassanio's tucket sounds, and for a moment Portia is not merry. She is deeply moved, and when she says,

> This night methinks is but the daylight sick;
> It looks a little paler; 'tis the day
> Such as the day is when the sun is hid,

we understand her thought. She is a young maid, tremulously waiting for her lover, and he comes. His confident "We should hold day with the Antipodes, If you would walk in absence of the sun," helps her, and gives the cue for a light answer:

> Let me give light, but let me not be light . . .
> But God sort all. You are welcome home, my lord.

It is a perfect close. No protestation. Her "my lord" tells all. Her lovely welcome to Antonio has just the same simplicity and deep sincerity.

Meanwhile Nerissa is not wasting time. She has begun to quarrel. Here is Gratiano, swearing by the moon and blustering about "the paltry ring," the "posy" and its value, while Nerissa, in her element, protests, "God is my judge."

But Portia by this time is ready, and she takes control. Her handling of Bassanio is perfect. She enjoys her jest, but speaks no word that leaves a sting. Bassanio responds. He has the dignity that Gratiano lacks. If Portia swears by heaven, he can swear, and can swear truly, by his honour.

> No, by mine honour, madam, by my soul . . .
> What shall I say, sweet lady?
> I was enforc'd to send it after him.
> I was beset with shame and courtesy;
> My honour would not let ingratitude
> So much besmear it. Pardon me, good lady.

At that, I think, she glows. Every word he says confirms her love and her essential faith in him, no matter what may be his faults. For do but note, dear critic (as Lorenzo might have put it), if you think with Q., but not with Granville Barker, of this young man as "a fortune-hunter, hypocrite and worse," that he was chosen by Antonio from all the youth of Venice because in the young profligate he saw a quality that others lacked. That is why he loved him and believed in him and said, before he knew the Belmont enterprise:

> I pray you, good Bassanio, let me know it,
> And if it stands, as you yourself still stand,
> Within the eye of honour, be assured
> My purse, my person, my extremest means
> Lie all unlock'd to your occasions.

Bassanio is a man. He tells the truth, and Portia loves him for it. But she means to test him once again, well knowing he will stand the test.

Gratiano's coarseness interrupts. Antonio at last breaks silence.

I am the unhappy subject of these quarrels.

Beautifully Portia meets him. "Grieve not you. You are welcome notwithstanding." But Bassanio, his nerves on edge, with something of his old less happy rhetoric, swears "by thine own fair eyes, Wherein I see myself . . ."

She will not let that pass—"Swear by your double self . . ." That ends his protestations.

Pardon this fault, and by my soul I swear
I never more will break an oath with thee.

Antonio himself, the friend who once "did lend his body" for this youth, now says, "I dare be bound again. My soul upon the forfeit."

What remains? Portia herself, having played out her comedy, outfacing and outswearing, till Bassanio has asked for pardon, tells the truth and asks for his. She gives the ring back by his friend's hand with a gesture which assures us, were assurance needed, that for her sweet spirit marriage will not mean possessiveness or breaking of old ties. She prayed for happiness in wedlock. She will have it. She has music in herself.

So, with good news for good Antonio, and good news too for Jessica—who also, we remember, "slandered her love, and he forgave it her," the spoken music ends with dignity in a procession to the house as morning breaks—except that, to remind us we are still on earth and not in heaven, Gratiano takes his chance, the moment Portia's back is turned, of giving us another taste of his good-humoured, harmless bawdry, very shocking to the Cambridge editors.

Such patterning as this our poets—or at any rate the best of them—have learnt both indirectly and directly in a long apprenticeship to Greek and Latin which began when Theodore, a Greek of Tarsus, founded our first Grammar Schools. Nor is it only in the formal pattern and the language that a master-craftsman's work blends gifts from Greece and Italy and Palestine. Here, for example, to the thought, Pythagoras and Plato, Cicero and Virgil have contributed as well as our own Chaucer.

I do not mean that Shakespeare imitated ancient poets, nor even that he rummaged among books like rare Ben Jonson and some modern Alexandrians. Nevertheless for us, a little rummaging does sometimes help.

The song that Hesiod learnt in old Boeotia from the Muses seemed to him an echo of a nobler music sung before the throne of Zeus, the Father of all gods and men. Was that the truth? Or was it somehow "like the truth?" It was a song which told of the emergence from primeval emptiness

and darkness of a better order through a mystery
of Love and Strife.

The generations passed. The great Ionian
speculators, though they often scoffed at Hesiod
and Homer, were poets, not logicians merely.
When Anaximander said, all things must pass
away to that from which they came, and "pay,
according to the ordinance of Time, the penalty
and compensation to each other for injustice," he
was certainly not postulating a monotonous unpur-
posed causal series, but a pattern of events in
nature, fit to be the source and sanction of our
human fumbling after "justice"; and a much
greater man, Pythagoras, in whom, as Cornford
said, commanding intellect was matched by deep
religious insight, thought the love of wisdom (*philosophia* he called it, modestly, not *sophia*) should be
a search not only for the laws revealed by mathematics, music and astronomy, but for a way of life.[1]
The mystery of numbers seemed to him a clue to
the significance of life itself, and in the heart's
response to music, beauty, loving kindness, he dis-
cerned a hint and promise of a spiritual harmony,
attainable by souls, and even by communities of
souls, responsive to the element of order and of
beauty in the world—for which the symbol is "the
music of the spheres." [2]

He thought, as men of science must (in logic,

[1] Jaeger, *Paideia*, vol. i, p. 158.
[2] F. M. Cornford, in *Cambridge Ancient History*, vol. iv, chapter xv,
vii, pp. 544 ff., and now in his beautiful essay on "The Music of the
Spheres" (*The Unwritten Philosophy*, Cambridge, 1950).

anyhow) that somehow in some sense life must
make sense; and nowadays no wise man scoffs at
him for that. As a revered and gracious thinker,
Alfred Whitehead, wrote in 1925:[1]

The field is open for the introduction of some new doctrine
of organism which may take the place of the materialism with
which since the seventeenth century, science has saddled
philosophy . . . We have come back to the doctrine of old
Pythagoras, from whom mathematics (in the modern sense), and
mathematical physics took their rise. He discovered the importance of dealing with abstractions, and in particular directed
attention to number as characterising the periodicity of notes in
music . . . In the twentieth century we find physicists largely
engaged in analysing the periodicity of atoms. Truly Pythagoras, in founding European philosophy and European mathematics, endowed them with the luckiest of lucky guesses—or was it
a flash of divine genius, penetrating to the inmost nature of things?

Though few philosophers and even fewer poets
can have understood Pythagorean logic and its
implications, his conception of a universal harmony
has lived, and has inspired great poetry in many
generations.

What exactly he himself said of the music of
the heavens or spheres, we do not know, nor does
it greatly matter. Certainly he spoke sometimes
as a poet and a prophet, not as a mere calculator.
That is why his teaching in the popular tradition
lived and lives as poetry—"There is one Harmony
of all things singing and quiring together in the
heavens which gives the universe in very truth the
name of Order." So the author of the treatise
"About Kosmos," once attributed to Aristotle,
puts it.

[1] *Science and the Modern World*, pp. 53 f.

Plato too was speaking as a poet—he himself admits it—when he told the story of the man Er,[1] who was twelve years in a trance, and woke to bring us news of his soul's journey to a meadow where he talked with other souls about their destiny, then travelled on till he beheld a pillar, stretched from earth to heaven, of light, and in the midst of it the spindle of Necessity, with its concentric circles, eight of them, carrying the stars, and on the rim of each a Siren, uttering one note, the whole eight making up a "harmony" or scale, while the three Fates sang to that music, one about the past, one of the present, and the other of the future.

"No," said Aristotle, that good man of common sense, uncommon shrewdness and invincibly keen observation, diligence and curiosity. "It isn't true. If people think the music's there, unheard, because we are so used to it, that like a blacksmith in his forge, we don't hear anything, that argument won't do. If there were really any music there would certainly be other consequences than just sound, effects, vibrations, we could note and measure. No, there's nothing in the fancy."

Milton discussed that view of the whole matter in a speech at Cambridge which refutes the vulgar error that he was a gloomy undergraduate. He states the argument of Aristotle very seriously, then exclaims, "How unimaginative! How could Aristotle think Pythagoras intended this delight-

[1] *Republic*, x, 614 ff.

ful fancy to be taken as prosaic fact?" Then, having slightly shocked his audience by such irreverence to Aristotle's high authority, the young man smiled (I think he smiled), and added, "After all, why shouldn't it be true?"

The fancy lived, and happily for all of us, when Cicero began to fail, or seem to fail, in politics, he gave us his best gift of all by his translation and interpretation for the use of Italy and Europe of the Greek philosophy he loved. We have lived on it, thanks to him. To all Europe in the Middle Ages and Renaissance he gave Scipio's Dream.

He told how Scipio, the Younger, having talked far on into the night with his host, an African chief, about his father, by adoption, the great Africanus, dreamt that his father came to him and prophesied for him a life of action, holding out the promise of the bliss reserved for faithful servants of the State. They live in spite of death. They have escaped the prison of the body. Scipio wept. "Why should I stay on earth to toil and suffer?" His father kissed him, and replied, "We must not be deserters; look about you!" He looked and saw. They were in a circle of bright light, the Milky Way, and the earth far below looked small, the Roman Empire a mere speck. He was ashamed, and then his father spoke again. "How long will you keep your mind fixed on the earth? Do you not see into what sacred precincts you have come? The whole is woven of wheels or spheres of which one is celestial, embracing all,

the Highest God . . . below are seven; in the
lowest is the moon, and below that is nothing that
is not mortal, perishable, save the minds and souls
of men." He gazed as in a trance, and, when he
was himself again, he said, "What is this sound
so loud and sweet that fills my ears?" "It is the
sound made by the impulse and the motions of
the spheres (*impulsu et motu orbium conficitur*), a
sound compact of various unequal intervals which
keep distinction in proportion."

Shakespeare remembered that. "There's not
the smallest orb but in his motion sings." The
Dream of Scipio was in those days a favourite
school text, for construe and for comment and
for declamation. It was got by heart, we may be
sure, by many boys to be exploited in their essays.

Another favourite school text was Virgil's sixth
book of the *Aeneid*, and we are on sure ground
when we say that Shakespeare knew and loved it.
No contemporary English version catches Virgil's
music as he did. The discourse of Anchises to
Aeneas in Elysium delighted him (vi, 724 ff.).
There are several echoes of it in our scene:

> Such harmony is in immortal souls,
> But whilst this muddy vesture of decay
> Doth grossly close it in, we cannot hear it . . .

and again,

> It is because your spirits are attentive.

> *Spiritus intus alit . . . quantum non corpora noxia tardant,*
> *Igneus est ollis vigor et coelestis origo*
> *Seminibus . . .*

As Dryden put it, several generations later:

> Heaven and Earth's compacted form
> And flowing waters and the starry flame,
> And both the radiant lights, one common soul
> Inspires and feeds and animates the whole . . .
> The aetherial vigour is in all the same,
> And every soul is filled with equal flame;
> As much as earthy limbs and gross allay
> Of mortal members subject to decay
> Blunt not the beams of heaven and edge of day.
> From this coarse mixture of terrestrial parts
> Desire and fear by turn possess their hearts,
> And grief and joy; nor can the grovelling mind
> In the dark dungeon of the limbs confined
> Assert the native skies or own its heavenly kind.

Shakespeare's reminiscence gave us something finer, more Virgilian in spirit, even than that.

In the more poignant scene which ends the tragedy of Cleopatra we hear an even nobler echo of that same Virgilian music.

> Give me my robe. Put on my crown. I have
> Immortal longing in me. Now no more
> The juice of Egypt's grape shall moist this lip.
> . . . Husband, I come:
> Now to that name my courage prove my title!
> I am fire and air; my other elements
> I give to baser life.

She is Queen of Egypt still, but something more. The robe and crown—the vesture and the garland—are symbols of the blest initiate's readiness for immortality. The cup is drunk and the wine tasted: the soul is ready, purged by the ordeal of every baser element.

> *quisque suos patimur manis . . .*
> *donec longa dies, prefecto temporis orbe*

150

concretam exabmit labem, purumque relinquit
aetherium sensum atque aurai simplicis ignem.

> I am fire and air; my other elements
> I give to baser life.

So rich, so various and so august is the tradition. Boethius in prison, Alfred, toiling for the education of his people, dreamt of the celestial music and the listening soul which can discern, however fitfully, the breath of heaven. So did Chaucer, Spenser, Shakespeare. So of course did Milton, whose *Ode on the Nativity* is loved, I think, especially because it blends in almost perfect harmony the loveliness and the essential truth both of the pagan and the Christian intuition. For him the prayer,

> Ring out, ye Crystall sphears,
> Once bless our human ears,
> If ye have power to touch our senses so . . .
> And with your ninefold harmony
> Make perfect consort to th'angelike symphony,

seems for the moment answered,

> For if such holy song
> Enwrap our fancy long,
> Time will run back and fetch the Age of Gold.

To every poet that is true, or like the truth.

> But wisest Fate says No,
> It must not yet be so,
> The Babe lies still in smiling infancy
> That on the bitter cross
> Must redeem our loss;
> So both himself and us to glorifie.

As many in our generation have discovered, there is truth in that as well.

151

MILTON'S CAMBRIDGE
EXERCISES

In war-time, at a College Quincentenary, a young man asked Lord Keynes, "Why make a fuss about these old traditions?" Keynes answered with a smile, "Because we think it important to be in love with the past and with the future." That was the clue. "To serve the future and deserve the past."

So Milton thought. "When God is decreeing to begin some new and great period, even to the reform of reformation itself . . . what does He then but reveal Himself to His servants, and, as His manner is, first to His Englishmen? I say, as His manner is, first to us, though we mark not the method of His counsels and are unworthy."

That is a *deo gratias* and *nostra culpa*, no vain boast but a challenge, a thanksgiving and a warning. Had we marked "the method of His counsels," or, in more prosaic terms, the facts of our career, since Caesar landed (to be followed by Augustine and by Theodore of Tarsus) we shouldn't be content to see the Classics languish in our universities, to label Latin "for Arts Students only," or to plan our "modern" schools, to which the great majority of boys and girls must go, on the assumption that no foreign language need be studied there at all. Let us enthrone by all means English as the Queen of the Humanites, but not forget how she became a Queen. Her diadem will tarnish and her reign be short if she becomes a slut or harridan. Not English studies only will wither and grow soft or feverish for lack of sap, if we deny our children access to the inspiration which has flowed throughout our history from Greece and Palestine and Rome.

It is no credit to our English scholarship that we have waited for a learned and acute American professor, Mr. T. W. Baldwin of Illinois, to rediscover and reveal the debt that Shakespeare owed to Stratford Grammar School, and for another eminent American, Professor D. L. Scott, to edit Milton's Cambridge Exercises, or Prolusiones (for the first time since their author published them in 1674) in the Columbia edition, with the imprint New York, 1936. These seven brilliant speeches, delivered when the poet was at Christ's, between the ages of sixteen and twenty-three, are the capital evidence for his personality and outlook at the time when he composed his early poems. Mrs. Tillyard's pleasant English version and Dr. Tillyard's commentary (1931) are a boon—but only the original can fully show the poet's ingenuity, variety and wit; only the Latin, as delivered in the Hall, the Schools, the Chapel, shows conclusively how happy, really happy, Milton was at Christ's.

He was a boy of sixteen, sensitive, precocious,

scholarly, but still a boy, when he received a letter, written in good Greek, from his friend Diodati—so well named, God's gift to him— suggesting a day's walk and talk together, though the weather looked unpromising—

I want your company so much, my wishful thinking makes me dream and almost prophesy fair weather for to-morrow, calm and everything that's golden ... Everything is going to be beautiful, air, sun, river, trees, birds, earth. Mere mortals, while we two make holiday, will laugh and dance for us. Heaven pardon my presumption!

We can imagine how the boy who found that letter, perhaps beside the truckle-bed from which he scrambled into shoes and gown for chapel— 5 a.m. in those days—raced across the court. How gray the clouds looked! How he thrilled with hope that yonder gleam upon the gray meant sunshine later.

Somewhere about this time that boy stood up in Hall and spoke prose-poetry. The occasion was a normal College Disputation, but his speech in praise of Day and mock disparagement of Night was memorable, for it was a prelude to the high poetical debate which gave us both L'Allegro and Il Penseroso, and which later, when his days and nights were dark, haunted his music still.

He began with a surprising version of a stock rhetorical commonplace, as old as Aristotle—

Gentlemen, a speaker at the outset should secure the good will of his audience. Unhappily I have to break that rule.

Solemnly he said it, but he meant his audience

154

to smile. The learned, who know not the ways of undergraduates, miss half the fun.

Such is the melancholy animosity between the devotees of different sorts of study, I see hostile faces all around me. Some look friendly just a few, and they more precious than the massed battalions of the dull and ignorant who pride themselves on the ridiculous and frothy effervescence of their own verbosity, but, when they have exhausted their stock phrases and their shreds and patches from new-fangled authors, they have not one word to say. They are struck dumb, as dumb as frogs are in Seriphos.

The frogs of that little island puzzled ancient amateur zoologists. They never croaked.

With all due deference, I don't think Milton joked with difficulty here, or thought himself unpopular, or heaped fresh fuel on a smouldering quarrel with his tutor. Surely Mr. Chappell smiled, when suddenly he changed his tone—

I beg your pardon, gentlemen. If I have spoken over-harshly, over-bitterly, forgive me, even those who have sworn deadly enmity against me. I confess I did it of set purpose.

How they must have laughed and cheered. When the tumult and the shouting died, came this triumphant explanation—

I did it of set purpose, for I wanted this, my speech in praise of Day to start like the first gleam of dawn under a cloudy sky, for that's the harbinger of sunshine later . . . I hold Day for the eldest daughter of Heaven, or rather of His Son, begotten by Him, it is said, to be the comfort of the race of men, the dread of the infernal gods, lest Night should rule unchallenged.

The long years passed. The poet, blind, almost defeated, still remembered.

I sung of Chaos and Eternal Night,
Taught by the Heavenly Muse to venture down

The dark descent and up to reascend . . .
Hail, Holy Light, offspring of Heaven first-born,
Or of the Eternal Co-eternal Beam . . .
Since God is Light.

When he was nineteen, Milton was elected "Father of the Revels" for the annual College merry-making in the Hall. He was delighted. Who could possibly take seriously his pretence that on returning home from London, "crammed with all the good things that are so abundant there," he had been torn from books against his will to take part in the Feast of Fools? In his high good humour he has compliments for all, "You, gentlemen, in whom the Muses are incarnate" and a sly thrust for himself—"Such fools as rail on other people's subjects, just because they couldn't ever master them—logic for instance." With a formidable list of classical examples he insists that jest and jollity are an essential part of a sound education. As for bearded Masters who shake stubborn heads in disapproval, he assures them—"Discipline was needed in their time. We are so much more diligent, for us some relaxation is imperative." Finally, after mischievous allusion to a popular young tough, apparently sent down for leading fifty young men "armed with stubby staves across the Barnwell Field to sabotage the aqueduct," he greets the guests, who, like the ancient hero, Jason, or the Knights of the Round Table, have braved the janitors and forced their way into the College.

At that point a medieval pageant enters: first,

two stalwart College servants—one a Mr. Spark, who comes in for some broad but kindly chaff— then youths, disguised as animals, who carry in the courses of an old-time College feast—first, third-year men, "boars pickled in beer these three years, but still tough enough to blunt your dog-teeth"; then "oxen roasted by Spark—and see! their gravy has run down into the pan" (one wonders if these lads have had some altercation with the porters, not without bloody noses?); then calves' head with no brains in them, kids, lean from keeping company with Venus . . . then birds, and, for dessert, a group of freshmen, "gallows-fruit, unripe medlars, still in need of hanging in the sun."

The pageant ended, Milton gaily (surely not at all distressed) disclaims his College nickname, Lady. "You call me Lady? Look at my ten sons! Who dares cast doubt on my virility?" With a delightful irony, he, the old rebel against Chappell's logic, has chosen that the masque this evening shall present the characters of Aristotle's dialectic. He himself is Ens, True Being, Father of the Categories.

He bids his sons keep sober, introduces them, and then—the miracle—

Hail, Native Language . . .

This incident was the fulfilment of the prayer of William Byngham, who, because he grieved at the decay of Grammar Schools, founded God's

House as a training school for teachers, then, in 1446, with good King Henry's help, founded Christ's College. In the Statutes he declared that after logic, the intending teacher should go back to grammar in the best sense of the word—that is to poetry, to Virgil and the rest.

That was the seed. This was the fruit. "The Latin speeches ended, the English thus began." How much more eloquent are Milton's famous lines if that mysterious, tantalizing phrase in our editions is explained.

Much of the thought in the familiar lines is Greek. The image of the poet's notions waiting to be clothed in language comes from Pindar [1] that of the lady searching in her wardrobe from the *Iliad*,[2] and the whole poem is a symphony in which words and thoughts from Greece and Rome and England make up a melodious English harmony for our delight.

What Milton says here isn't simply that he is ambitious to write epic, but that he has a vision of a poet's pilgrimage through life. The Mind soars and the poet hears some strain of an immortal music; then, because he is no more, nor less than human, he must pass through fire and mist and cold and storms until at last the Mind returns to our dear Mother Earth and reads the secrets of the Beldame, the Fair Lady, Nature. But the pilgrimage has not been wasted. Here at home are Kings and Queens and Heroes, and the poet here

[1] *Pyth.* i, 8.   [2] *Il.* v, 286 ff.

makes music, harmony, to hold "sad souls and all the rest" enchanted.

This description of the poet's voyage of discovery is the best clue to the interpretation of the speeches in which Milton criticizes the old barren logic and its failure to evoke the impulse for acquiring or provide the leisure for digesting knowledge, and contrasts it with his own conception of a richer, more imaginative diet.

How much better it would be, Academicians, and how much more worthy of that name, to visit and survey, as on a map, the countries of the world; to travel in imagination through regions made illustrious by wars and triumphs and by tales that famous poets tell; to cross the surging Adriatic and approach unscathed the flames of Aetna; to take notice of men's customs, and the beautifully ordered governments of peoples, and after that search out and thoroughly explore the nature of all creatures that have breath; then bid the Mind descend to contemplate the secret properties of stones and plants. And, O my hearers, do not hesitate to soar into the heavens, and there observe the manifold cloud-shapes, the high-heaped snow-packs and the source from which the dews, the tears of morning, flow. Then peep into the boxes where the hail is stored, inspect the arsenal of thunderbolts, nor let it be to you a secret what Jupiter or Nature hath in view when a grim comet ever and anon threatens the sky with conflagration. Nor should *you* miss one tiny star, no, not the tiniest however many there may be, dispersed and wandering between the poles. Nay, follow with the Sun as the companions of his journey and call Time himself to render an account. Compel him to divulge the plan of his unending march. But more—don't let your Mind consent to be hemmed in and fenced about by the same boundaries to which the world conforms. Nay, let it wander far beyond the ramparts of the universe and learn at last the crowning lesson of Self-Knowledge, and therewith acquaintance with those Sacred Minds and high Intelligences with whom presently it is to enter into everlasting comradeship.

Milton aims higher than the pious founders of

the Royal Society itself. He doesn't say, with Bishop Sprat, "Two subjects, God and the Soul, being foreborne." On the contrary, for him the soul is the hero of all educational adventure. The process is the mind's instruction, the goal, self-knowledge such as fits the spirit for its proper destiny.

When he used the word Academicians at the outset Milton thought of Plato. Then he thought of Bacon, but it was a poet's rapture, not the quest of the experimental man of science he described. Finally his thought returned to Greece. What could be more important than the lessons history, geography and sociology and natural philosophy can teach? Self-knowledge, the old Delphic and Socratic "Know thyself," thus reinterpreted— such knowledge as can fit the spirit for acquaintance here and comradeship hereafter with immortal souls?

That is the theme pursued by Milton in the Seventh Discourse, spoken just before he went away from Cambridge, in the College Chapel. Those who talk of Hubris miss the meaning. Milton's belief was not that cleverness or learning, without character, can help us, nor that man's unaided genius, without grace, can give a foretaste of apotheosis. But he does believe that man's capacity and thirst for knowledge are a proof that search into the ways of nature is his bounden duty in the service of God's praise. The intricacy of the great design does not, for him, refute the notion that the whole was made for man; rather, the universe was thus created that man's mind, by searching out its secrets, might become what God intended Man to be. That is what he means when he declares:

Your spirit, hearers, when at last the cycle of all knowledge is completed, a slave no longer in this prison-house of toil and gloom, will so extend its reach, through the expansion of a certain greatness, as to embrace the universe, nay, space beyond. Then will most accidents and consequences be at length made so immediately clear that to the master of this citadel of wisdom nothing in his life can happen by mere chance, nothing for which he cannot make provision. He will seem an emperor whose rule the stars obey, whom land and sea both serve, and storm-winds wait upon his pleasure; one to whom our Parent Nature hands in her submission, just as if some divinity had laid aside his rule over the world and had entrusted all its rights, its laws, its government to Man as Viceroy.

The voice may seem the voice of a belated Marlowe, but the meaning is not Marlowe's. It is a minister, not God Himself, who makes the man of science viceroy over causes and effects in this material world. Man is a pilgrim still. On strict terms only, by the use of all his faculties, he can make progress, far beyond the reach of our imagination. Even so, there is a higher destiny reserved for him hereafter, when the soul, restored to its true nature, shall return to God.

The Artist of the Universe, though He subjected all things else to flux and to decay, mingled with whatsoever part of Man is mortal something of Himself, a breath divine ... and this, when it had sojourned pure and stainless here awhile, a pilgrim and celestial guest, He meant should mount on wings up to his native sky and there be gathered to its fatherland, its rest. Nothing may therefore be accounted as among the causes of our happiness that hath not in some way regard both to that life eternal and to this, our life as citizens on earth.

We are reminded of the Cambridge Platonists, Whichcote to whom religion was "a seed of a deiform nature," and Henry More, who entered Christ's from Eton just about the time when Milton preached this Discourse in the Chapel.

When all is said, it is the poetry which is immortal and irrefutable, "true, or somehow like the truth." When Milton spoke about the music of the spheres he laughed at Aristotle for supposing Plato and Pythagoras believed such music could be heard in fact, then turned on him and asked: "Why shouldn't it be true?" The combination of the Christian and the pagan symbolism in his poetry was not a marriage made by logic, but by free imagination. In the Ode he wrote on Christmas Eve at Christ's he dreamt that Nature had herself believed her task, her reign was ended when the Christ, the perfect Man, was born. But wisest Fate said no. The Tempter must be foiled, the crucifixion, resurrection, judgment, must be all accomplished, before that "greater Man," with whom His own shall then be one, takes up the reins to rule.

So Milton sang, then went out to his own part in the fight, and failed. Or did he fail? At any rate, the Heavenly Muse, the Spirit, never ceased to visit him with memories and hopes of beauty. Was it only wishful thinking that made Diodati "dream and almost prophesy" fair weather for the morning?

THE PRESIDENT OF THE IMMORTALS

Tess of the D'Urbervilles is the story of a woman, sensitive, impulsive, ignorant, deflowered in youth, and her life ruined, by a man whom at the end, perplexed in the extreme, she kills. Hardy has told it faithfully, with deep compassion, shirking no tragic issue, moulding the crude material in a pattern which recalls the scope and beauty of Greek tragic poetry, but using as his instrument an exquisitely modulated prose. Perhaps no tale in living memory has helped so much to make hearts kinder, men and women just a little wiser and society less cruel. Yet it was greeted when it first appeared with cries of "blasphemous," "indecent," "coarse," "immoral," and strange things were said of Hardy, some in good faith, some unpardonable things in malice. Hardy, bewildered by the clamour, over-sensitive, perhaps, but deeply hurt, tried vainly to explain. He was an artist and he wrote "impressions," true, he hoped (at any rate poetically true), to life as he had seen it, not *ex cathedra* pronouncements on theology or morals. When a second hue and cry was raised about his *Jude*, he gave up writing prose. In verse, he sadly told himself, he could write frankly, and perhaps without offence. Had Galileo said in verse that the world moved, "the Inquisition might have left him alone."

What after all was his offence? First, he had dared to take a "fallen" woman as his heroine, and call her "a pure woman," on his title-page. But there was worse than this. In summing up her tragedy he wrote these fatal words:

"Justice" was done, and the President of the Immortals (in Aeschylean phrase) had ended his sport with Tess.

Torn from its context, misapplied and misinterpreted that sentence was enough. Hardy, his critics said, had represented God as a malignant, wanton jester, all-powerful and endowed with the baser human passions, who turns everything to evil and rejoices in the mischief. To Hardy, one such critic still maintained, some thirty years after the book appeared, "evil is not so much a mystery, a problem, as the wilful malice of his god." "Such ludicrous opinions," Hardy answered, "I do not hold and never have held. They are really or approximately those of the primitive believer in his man-shaped, tribal god."

One thing the critics failed to notice, or conveniently ignored. The first three words of the offending sentence were a challenge, not to the First Cause, but to themselves. "Justice" was done, our necessary, but imperfect human "Justice." The law took its course. Tess had killed Alec and was hanged for it. For that at any rate we and the institutions we inherit, and in part control, must take responsibility. To-day, in all the circumstances, Tess might well have been reprieved, to suffer what the law, as now administered, accounts a penalty more merciful. The challenge to our conscience still remains. It is essentially the Christian challenge: "He that is without sin, let him cast the first stone"; and Shakespeare's challenge too: "God's bodikin, man, much better. Use every man after his desert and who shall 'scape whipping?"

But there is more than that implied in this first phrase. What is the context?

A little while ago, in the last watch of the night, Tess lay asleep at Stonehenge, in a precinct haunted by memories of ancient, cruel superstition. Her husband, Angel Clare, kept watch. Towards the dawn, the ministers of Law closed in for her arrest. "Let her finish her sleep," he begged, and they consented. He bent over her, holding one little hand. Then, as the morning light grew stronger, a ray fell on her and she woke . . . "What is it, Angel? Have they come for me?" "Yes, dearest, they have come." "It is as it should be," she murmured. "Angel, I am almost glad—yes, glad. This happiness could not have lasted. It was too much. I have had enough, and now I shall not live for you to despise me . . ." She stood up, shook herself, and went forward, neither of the men having moved. "I am ready," she said quietly.

The readiness is all. Tess herself makes no complaint. Quietly, "almost glad—yes, glad," she goes.

We are reminded surely of Greek tragedy, of a Cassandra, victim of Apollo's lust and jealousy, of man-made war and Agamemnon's cruelty as well. Greeting the house of death, she enters, bravely, quietly, with pity in her heart: [1]

> Alas for mortal lives, their happiness
> A shadow-picture; their adversity
> A sketch at the touch of a wet sponge dashed out;
> And this I pity more.

We are reminded too perhaps of Hecuba, greeting with joy the messenger who comes to tell her that her child is dead, because she thinks she is to die as well: [2]

Talthybius. Where is the sometime Queen of Ilion?
Chorus. Prostrate and shrouded in her robe she lies.
Talthybius. O Zeus, what shall I say? Dost thou regard
Mankind? Or are the gods an idle dream,
And Fortune the sole ruler . . .?
This was the Queen of golden Troy, the wife
Of happy Priam. I would rather die
Than live to be the sport and scorn of Fortune
As she is. Poor disconsolate, rouse yourself.
Hecuba. Why, who is this, that will not leave my body
In peace? Let grief lie still, whoe'er you be.
Talthybius. I am Talthybius, and I serve the Greeks.
Hecuba. The Greeks! Oh, will they sacrifice me too?
Then, welcome, friend. You bring me welcome news.
Let us make haste . . .

"Let her finish her sleep," said Angel, and

[1] *Agamemnon*, 1326 ff.   [2] Euripides, *Hecuba*, 484–507.

Tess, waking, murmured, "It is as it should be
. . . I am almost glad . . . I am ready."

Presently Angel stood with Liza-Lu, her sister, on the hill-side,
watching for the signal from the prison, which would tell them it
was finished. Slowly, silently, the black flag climbed the mast.
"Justice" was done, and the President of the Immortals . . .

The transition, the implied appeal, from human
courts of justice to the gods is beautiful and moves
us. But what of the Aeschylean phrase? Is it a
flourish, an evasion, a parade, in doubtful taste, of
scholarship? On the contrary, it is a clue to
Hardy's deepest thought. In August 1889, when
he was settling down at Dorchester to write this
book, he had been reading Aeschylus, and made
this "casual note," quoted by Mrs. Hardy in the
Life (vol. I, p. 289):

When a married woman who has a lover kills her husband, she
does not really wish to kill the husband; she wishes to kill the
situation. Of course in Clytaemnestra's case, it was not exactly
so . . .

Nor is it, in the case of Tess, "exactly so." But
Tess was surely in his mind when, eight months
earlier (on December 10, 1888) he wrote:

He, she had blundered; but not as the Prime Cause had
blundered. He, she had sinned; but not as the Prime Cause
had sinned. He, she was ashamed and sorry, but not as the
Prime Cause would be ashamed and sorry if it knew.

So when he wrote the book, he chose the
Aeschylean phrase as a reminder of the deep sincerity and compassion with which Aeschylus, the
greatest of the Greek religious poets, sought to

reconcile the facts of human suffering and sin with his unconquerable hope, or vision, of a righteous order in the universe. The tragic discord, and the faith which seeks (not always quite in vain) its resolution, are implicit even in the thought of Homer, when he spoke of Hector's tragedy and of the Wrath, with all its consequences, as "fulfilment of the Will of Zeus":

Go thou apart . . . I promise it, these things shall be my care.

Hardy remembered that, I think, when, as the title for the final movement of his tragedy, he chose the word "Fulfilment."

Anyhow, Aeschylus remembered it, when he made Clytaemnestra pray, with an appalling irony,

> Zeus, Zeus, Accomplisher, fulfil my prayer.
> What Thou intendest to accomplish be Thy care,[1]

and when he set that prayer for vengeance that can only breed fresh trouble in sharp contrast to the meditation of the Chorus:

> Zeus, whosoe'er he be . . . I weigh the world and find
> Save Zeus no other helper if the mind
> Oppress'd so strangely is to lift the burden and be free.[2]

Even more relevant to Hardy's thought of Tess is the appeal, in the first play we have from Aeschylus, the *Suppliants*, of those poor hunted women, victims of the lust and cruelty of their own kinsmen, who, like Tess, perplexed in the

[1] *Agamemnon*, 964 f.   [2] *Agamemnon*, 170 ff.

extreme, cry out to heaven—but seem to cry in vain: [1]

1st Voice. O that the Will of Zeus—
2nd Voice. The Will of Zeus?
Nay, that is hard to track.
Though everywhere His light
Glimmer against the night,
No mortal eye can read
Fate's flickering Chance, and still our night is black.

1st Voice. The doom by Zeus decreed,
Once by His Nod confirmed, falleth aright,
Thrown by no wrestler—

2nd Voice. Blind
The secrets of His mind,
As overgrown with weeds,
Pathways in thickets, lost to human sight.

1st Voice [or Full Chorus?].
From Hope's ambitious height
He hurleth men away,
Needing no weapon for the fight
Nor armour for the fray;
Only within His Mind, the Thought,
Whereby His Harmony is wrought;
No striving; on the eternal throne
He labours not, yet all is done.

Aeschylus here blends Homer's thought with the Pythagorean vision of a universal Harmony. The grounds on which these women claim the help of gods and men are, in the first place, their distress and helplessness, their need of pity, and the justice of their cause. But, by an irony of which the poet was acutely conscious, they make it their chief claim, both on the city of Argos and

---

[1] *Supplices,* 88–109. I accept the masterly interpretation of this noble passage given us by Walter Headlam in his *Book of Greek Verse* (Cambridge), 1907, pp. 277 ff.

on Zeus himself, that they are descended from an Argive princess, Io, who was long ago beloved by Zeus, and, as the victim of His passion and of Hera's jealousy, was changed from human shape, hunted and driven through the world in anguish, but at last restored. Made pregnant by the healing touch of Zeus and the in-breathing of His spirit became the mother of a hero, Epaphus, worshipped in Egypt as a god. This story has been clothed by Aeschylus with beauty, as the symbol of a mystery which almost, but not quite, redeems it from the ugliness and cruelty of its barbaric origin . . . Almost, not quite.

Their hymn begins, for instance, thus:[1]

> Steer of Zeus, we summon thee,
> Helper from beyond the sea;
> Io, in a flowery land
> Grazing, by the healing hand
> And the breath of Zeus conceiving,
> When the appointed months were run,
> Bore in that same sign a son,
> And she called him Epaphus,
> Offspring of the touch of Zeus;
>
> Therefore now we name thy name,
> Coming as our Mother came
> To these meadow-lands of old.
> So the story, here retold,
> Of the past with all its grieving,
> In the future days may bring
> More than Hope's imagining.
> What has been may be again,
> And the future make all plain.

[1] *Supplices*, 40 ff.

Birds are singing in the land.
Is there one can understand?
He will tell you, he will know—
'Tis the hawk-chased bride of woe,
Tereus' luckless bride, who wrought
Sorrow from a bitter thought,
The sweet nightingale, bereft,
Longing for the home she left,
Grieving in some leafy grove
And weaving a strange tale of love—
How love by hate to death was done
When a mother slew her son.

So in a sad Ionian strain,
We, like her, complain.
Tender, sun-ripe cheeks we mar;
Hearts that knew not grief are breaking;
And the flowers we gather are
Sighs for fear of love's forsaking—
From a dim and distant land,
Strangers, none to help or understand.

None but the gods! Give ear! Be just!
Let not youth and lust
Spurn the ordinance of grace,
Wanton in despite of measure.
Hear us, Author of our Race,
Save us from their sinful pleasure;
Shield us, ye whose altars are
A refuge, even after stress of war.

From that appeal they pass to the solemn meditation which I have already quoted. Then there
is a change of mood to bitterness and almost blind
despair—[1]

Such the burden of the sorrow we are fain to sing.
Tears are falling, voices crying, grief that knows no comforting.
Woe is me, alas, alas.

---

[1] 118 ff.

Bounis, Apia, holy, mountain-land!
Bounis, Apia, thou wilt understand
The stranger's uncouth wail,
The tearing of the raiment and the rending of the veil.
Gods in heaven, what thanksgiving have the dead to bring?
Gifts are given by the living. Death can make no offering.
Woe on woe, alas, alas!
Here's a coil past ravelling.
Where shall break the wave of sorrow.
Bounis, Apia, etc.

Then again they sing more calmly, but excitement grows until at last they rail upon the gods themselves and threaten self-destruction.[1]

The wind was fair, the oars well-plied,
And the frail bark that housed us made good way.
Fenced from the angry waters we defied
The storm of the pursuit. So now we pray,
The journey, well begun, may find
A port and haven not less kind.

A holy Mother's seed are we.
Keep us Virginal and free.
Never let the brute prevail.
Never mate us with the male.

Goddess of Virginity,
Guardian of the gates of yonder shrine,
From persecution's tyranny,
Child of Zeus, defend us, Maid divine.
As thou hatest rape and wrong,
From the fury of the strong,
Artemis enshrined,
Save us and be kind.

Or else this dark sun-smitten band
Will seek that other Zeus in dead-man's land,
The god who never turned a guest away:

---

[1] 140 ff.

And these strange garlands, we shall say,
So fast about our throats are tied,
Because the gods to whom we pray
Refused us, and we died.
Ah, Zeus! Woe upon woe!
The pangs of Io wake again in me.
Now, cruel Queen of Heaven, we understand
Thy triumph, and we know,
When winds blow from the land
There shall be storm at sea.

Then shall my reproach be heard.
"Zeus, thou art unjust," a bitter word.
"Behold thy children, born of Io's pain,"
Cry it aloud, and cry again,
"Behold the offspring of the steer,
Thy children, named thy name in vain."
    Look down, O Zeus, and hear.

That mood passes, and in the sequel for a time, it seems, their prayer is to be answered. Argos takes up their cause and fights for them. But in the event, their persecutors triumph, capture Argos, and force the women to a loveless marriage. On the fatal wedding-night all except one, the gentle Hypermnestra, killed their husbands. Hypermnestra spared her man, was put on trial for what seemed an act of treachery to Argos and the righteous cause. But Aphrodite intervened, and, in the name of nature's law, bade Argos honour her and hail her as the destined mother of a race of heroes.

Aeschylus meant us, I believe, to see in Hypermnestra's act of grace a hint, a promise, of the hope that somehow, in our human chaos, loving kindness will prevail, and a divine persuasion prove

a surer guide than violence and hate. But certainly
he knew, although he bowed in reverence before
the mystery, that, in the court of reason and of our
own conscience, he was far from having "justified"
in Milton's phrase, "the ways of God to Man."

After long happy years the merciful deliverance
of Greece through Athens in the Persian wars, and
the rebirth of Athens in fresh beauty and a new-
found generosity inspired him with the faith
expressed, and symbolized, by the conversion of
the Furies to Kind Goddesses. Yet he turned
again, in the *Prometheus*, to the same ultimate,
perhaps unanswerable question he had pondered
when he wrote the *Supplices*. Once more he
"faithfully presented" Io, victim of the lust of
Zeus and jealousy of Hera, driven through the
world in anguish, and yet destined in the end to
be by Zeus Himself restored. So had Prometheus
prophesied, the friend of man, who suffered for his
friendship, but who knew a secret that Zeus did
not know. "Which of the gods is so hard-
hearted," cry the Ocean Nymphs, "as to take
pleasure in such things? All share your suffering,
save Zeus . . ." "It shall yet come to pass,"
Prometheus answers, "that the President of the
Immortals (*makaron prutanis*) shall have need of
me, dire need to learn his lesson, for unless he
learns it, he must lose his throne." [1] The lesson
is of wisdom, mercy, self-control.

[1] *Prometheus Vinctus*, 180 ff. This was the immediate source of
Hardy's phrase, but he was thinking also of the *Supplices*.

To Aeschylus that seemed a possibility, perhaps a prophecy, of hope for Athens and mankind. Perhaps to Hardy also, when in later life, in the last movement of *The Dynasts*, he made the "Chorus of the Pities" sing:

A stirring fills the air
Like the sound of joyance there
That the rages
Of the Ages
Shall be cancelled, the deliverance offered for the darts that were,
Consciousness the Will informing till it fashion all things fair.

Certainly, it was not more than a hope for him, a hope not yet fulfilled. "But wisest Fate says no . . ." Wisest?

What of that last grim phrase: "The President . . . had ended his sport with Tess." That isn't Aeschylean. It is far more tragic even than the Aeschylean tale of Io and Prometheus. It is Gloster's thought (not Shakespeare's) in *King Lear*.

As flies to wanton boys are we to the gods;
They kill us for their sport.

Not Shakespeare's thought? What then did Shakespeare mean by making Gloster say it? The play's the thing. This is the context.

Gloster in lusty youth begot the traitor Edmund. He still boasts of it in his old age: "He came somewhat saucily into the world, yet his mother was fair. There was good sport at his making." Now, thanks to Edmund's villainy, Gloster is blind, an outcast, led he knows not and he cares not whither; but haunted always by one thought:

> Ah, dear son Edgar,
> Might I but live to see thee in my touch.
> I'd say I had eyes again.

Edgar, poor Tom, is present, though unrecognized, still caring for him, while he rails upon the gods.

Presently Edgar guides him to the cliff, saves him from suicide, and with him is a witness of the scene in which both son and father pity Lear more than themselves. The climax of that scene is Lear's "Kill, kill, kill!" After that Gloster speaks in a new tone:

> Ye ever gentle gods,
> Let not my worser spirits tempt me again
> To die before you please.

But even that is not the end. Soon we shall hear him say:

> No further, sir. A man may rot even here.

And again Edgar helps him.

> What? In ill thoughts again? Men must endure
> Their going hence, even as their coming hither.
> Ripeness is all. Come on.

Gloster.   And that's true too.

Slowly, silently, the black flag climbed the mast.

" Justice" was done, and the President of the Immortals (in Aeschylean phrase) had ended his sport with Tess. And the D'Urberville knights and dames slept on in their tombs unknowing. The two speechless gazers bent themselves down to the earth, as if in prayer, and remained thus a long time, absolutely motionless; the flag continued to wave silently. As soon as they had strength, they arose, joined hands again and went on.

That is the truth of the matter, faithfully presented. Tess had said, "I am almost glad—yes, glad, and I am ready." But we, the silent watchers, grieve for her, and so must all who love her. Now it is we, not she, who feel the irony of human justice, claiming such a victim, and the mystery of the Will, weaving, as it seems to us, so blindly circumstance with circumstance; and sometimes, naturally, we cry out with Gloster, shame upon the gods. And yet again we think, perhaps somehow, in part at any rate, the root is in ourselves: Tess was a D'Urberville. But at the close, the watchers bend themselves to earth, as if in prayer, rise up when strength returns, join hands again, and so pass on.

That is Sophoclean in effect. We remember Hyllus, following his father to the pyre, still grieving for his mother——[1]

Lift him, attendants. Understand what now I do, and so forgive. From this which here is done, know that the gods are harsh and do not understand . . . Go, maidens. Linger not. You have looked upon a strange sad death, and still you look on one who suffers terribly. Yet all these things are Zeus.

We think too of Antigone, and of the last words spoken to her, just before she goes her way to Thebes for her last loving sacrifice, alone.[2]

Lament no more. These things are so.

---

[1] *Trachiniae*, 1264 ff.   [2] *Oedipus at Colonus*, 1778 ff.

Hardy was also like Euripides in some ways. About many things he was uncertain, but of two things, certain—first, that cruelty is evil; secondly, that if the gods do evil they are not fit gods for a man's worship. For the rest he often echoes the Euripidean question:[1]

> Who hath knowledge? Who so wise
> Can tell us what divinities,
> Spirits of a mingled birth,
> Part of heaven, and part of earth,
> Shape our mortal destinies,
> Weaving in a web of chance
> Circumstance with circumstance?
> Veiled from mortals in conjecture vain
> Truth lies. The secrets of the gods remain.

Finally, we can listen, if we will, to Hardy's own voice, speaking to us, as it seemed to speak, out of the fire of life, to him:

> "You taught not that which you set about,"
> Said my own voice talking to me,
> "That the greatest of things is Charity."
> And the sticks burnt low, and the fire went out,
> And my voice ceased talking to me.[2]

If ever any man taught Charity, Thomas Hardy did.

---

[1] *Helena*, 1137 ff.
[2] From "Surview," the last poem printed in the Collected Edition, Macmillan, 1923.

THE CHARIOTEER

> Bring me my bow of burning gold,
> Bring me my arrows of desire,
> Bring me my spear—O clouds, unfold—
> Bring me my chariot of fire.

WHICH of these images is Greek, which Hebrew? The golden bow, the arrows of desire, are, I suppose, Greek; the prophet's chariot, I venture to suggest, both Greek and Hebrew.

But watch the faces of our English children, as they sing, half-understanding, but entranced:

> I will not cease from mental strife
> Nor shall my sword sleep in my hand,
> Till we have built Jerusalem
> In England's green and pleasant land.

Whether or not they and their teachers know it, their spirits are responsive to the inspiration which has come to us from Greece and Palestine.

When Socrates and Phaedrus met and talked together on the banks of Ilissus in the plane-tree's shadow where the breeze was gentlest, Socrates told his friend, as Robert Bridges puts it,[1]

> The vision of the seer who saw the spirit of Man.
> A chariot he beheld, speeding twixt earth and heaven,
> Drawn by winged horses, and the charioteer thereon
> Upright, with eyes upon the goal and mind alert,
> Controlling his strong steeds . . .

---

[1] *Testament of Beauty*, Book ii. Professor Beazley's phrase is quoted from his chapter on Greek Art and Architecture in the *Cambridge Ancient History*, vol. v, chapter xv, iii, p. 426.

One thinks of the bronze Charioteer at Delphi, which Plato must have seen—youth, ready for the race, resolved and quiet. He will drive well, intent, not heeding the crowd's fever. If he wins, he will be glad, and smile "a royal smile," to use Professor Beazley's perfect phrase, as when "deep spiritual felicity transfigures the face without perceptible change of feature."

So must Thrasyboulos, the young prince from Sicily, have looked when Pindar watched him in the race at Delphi, anxious for him, knowing well the danger of the course; and so he may have smiled, after the race was won, when he proclaimed his father as the victor. Pindar made a song to greet him as, acclaimed and garlanded, he drove his chariot that night in triumph to the symposium. "My friend," the poet said, "your father sent you here to win the race for him. It has been won. You have proclaimed him victor. Now my loving thought, my prayer for you, is this: May you, like young Achilles, learn the ancient Centaur's wisdom, honouring first Zeus and then your parents. This I dare to say. Your father has a son who willingly, if the need came, would, like Antilochus of old, lay down his life for him." [1]

Pindar wrote that about the time of Marathon, perhaps a little earlier. Twenty years later he still felt and said the same about this friend.

The Charioteer (*heniochos*, the "holder of the reins") in the Homeric battle had to wait, clear-

[1] Pindar, *Pythian*, vi.

headed, calm in face of danger, ready always to attempt a rescue, self-controlled and able to control his team. Sometimes he gave his life to save his master, as Antilochus did for Nestor, and often, in real life as well as poetry, such a young man as he has been a hero's wise and trusted friend—Horatio to Hamlet, as it were, Patroclus to Achilles. That was surely Homer's thought, and that was why he chose Antilochus to be the friend who runs in deep concern to tell Achilles, "Your Patroclus has been killed."

In ordering the funeral games, Achilles puts the chariot-race first, and says, "Had not these funeral games been for Patroclus, I should myself have taken part and won this race. My horses are immortal. But to-day they mourn for him, their charioteer, for he was kind to them, and he would wash them and anoint their manes with olive-oil."

We understand. The hero, waking slowly from the passion which has blinded him and made him less than human, is helped already by the memory of his friend's modest, quiet temper, and himself in the conduct of the games shows something of the same unruffled, gracious spirit. In that Antilochus helps. From the sage advice of Nestor to his son, "Your horses may be slow; but wits and skill, not brute strength, win," to the happy sequel when Achilles finds a special prize for Nestor, since his horses and his son have done so well, and he is too old to compete in other contests, the generous courtesy both of Achilles as the peacemaker and umpire, and of Antilochus as the most magnanimous of all competitors, delight and comfort us.[1]

The end is not yet. Though the cloud of his obsession lightens in the sunshine of this day, it will return. But when the poet says "Achilles smiled and he had pleasure in Antilochus, because he was his dear friend," we are assured that before long the hero, helped both by his mother's love and by his own deep reverence for Zeus, will "know himself" as Delphic wisdom in a later generation puts it.

The conception also of the charioteer, incautious, over-confident, whose horses bolt and wreck the chariot, involving him and others in disaster is proverbial. No mortal can control the horses of the Sun or drive his chariot and live— not even Phaethon, though he was half-divine and was beloved by gods and men.

Centuries passed. All Athens marvelled at the *Oresteia*. Over his mother's body stood Orestes, Delphi's minister and victim, hailed by many voices as a righteous liberator who has won the race of vengeance, but himself distracted, realizing for the first time what it was that he had done:[2]

> This victory, unenviable, unclean, I know not
> How it will end. My mind is like a team
> The driver cannot master, and I swerve
> A little from the course. I have a fear,

---

[1] *Iliad,* xvii, 640 ff., 685 ff.; xviii, 15–33; xxiii, 555–556 and 615 ff.
[2] *Choephoroe,* 1019 ff.

Ready to pipe at the heart, and the heart waits
Ready to dance at the tune . . .
While I am sane, let me speak.

Presently he sees the Furies.

To Plato's vision in the *Phaedrus* all these themes, traditional, familiar, have contributed. But there is yet another theme, suggested by Parmenides, the most austere logician of the ancient world.[1] It is perhaps a paradox but that does not surprise us in Parmenides—that he, who sought, and thought he found, the truth by a strict logic in denial of all motion, birth and growth, change and decay and death, wrote poetry (or anyhow wrote verse), and as a prelude to the exposition of his dismal creed, described a journey he had made from earth to heaven in a chariot, guided by the daughters of the Sun, out of gross darkness to the bright light of a perfect day, where One is One and all alone, and ever more shall be so. A brave adventure, one is bound to feel, but what a bleak discovery.

That logic too contributed to Plato's vision. Clouds unfold, horizons open to such honest thinkers. Plato's own sharp distinctions between flesh and spirit, his insistence on pure Reason, abstract, mathematical, have done some harm—especially as misinterpreted by persons, institutions, schools of thought and politics and churches, much less kind than Plato. All his myths are

[1] For a sympathetic account of Parmenides, both as a thinker and as a poet, see Jaeger, *Paideia*, vol. i, pp. 173 ff.

poetry—prose-poetry. Some people talk and act grim, very faulty prose. Plato himself, it is only fair to remember, tried to put us on our guard against that very thing.

Socrates believed the soul immortal. That makes all the difference. Prophets, poets, lovers and "initiates," "enthusiasts," perhaps have seen a vision and remember it, or part of it. They may be mad, we say—possessed, and very often they are dangerous. And yet sometimes, perhaps, the madness is divine.

Exactly what the soul is, Socrates admits, not he nor any one of us can tell. Only a god could know. What she is *like*—well, that's another matter. Shall we say, like a chariot, drawn by two horses, the embodiment of human passions, guided by Reason, a right noble charioteer? One of the horses is a thoroughbred, courageous, pricked by honour, spirited, ambitious, beautiful; the other is his opposite, the steed of appetite. To drive them is inevitably difficult and irksome, and mistakes are dangerous, and may be fatal.

What happens? When the gods drive out, Zeus first in his winged car, the other great gods in his wake—only the housewife Hestia (the hearth-goddess) left at home to keep house for the family and keep the home fires burning—the whole shining train is followed by the rest of the immortals: and as many other souls as wish may follow, even though they may be souls half-mortal or still mortal. All may join. There is no jealousy in the heavenly choir.

Plato knew something about choirs and places where they sing. There is no jealousy, we faintly hope. But there are difficulties. While the gods drive to the height in perfect balance, easily, with human souls inevitably it goes harder, since one of our steeds at any rate has evil in him and drags down the charioteer. Hence anguish and sometimes disaster.

Souls fare differently of course. Most of us fail to reach the height, but even these have glimpses, memories that help a little. Some whose charioteer is wisest, and his horses well controlled, may take some impress of the likeness of the gods, and so drive up and on until the driver's head is high enough for him to see, if only for a little while, pure truth and beauty, as they really are, beyond the edge of heaven itself. Most fail, and many fall, with horses maimed, wings broken, just because they jostle for a place and trample on each other, fighting to come first. All such depart, still uninitiated.

Such is the mystery of life and love, a vision here half apprehended, an aspiration and a striving; many, many failures. Even so, according to the poet, souls that fail may pass to other lives, each, in the measure of the aspiration or the failure, better or worse equipped for the next station of the pilgrimage. Those who have sought truth faithfully and loved a friend within the bounds of wisdom will fare best.

Such is the vision told by Socrates to Phaedrus and retold for us and our own age by Robert Bridges in his *Testament of Beauty*. Reading again the *Phaedrus* in the light of his interpretation we may learn perhaps to think a little better than did Plato of the steed which he thought evil. Both the steeds are good, not evil, but both wilful; both need expert management. So indeed, I fancy, does the Charioteer himself. Anyhow, walking and discoursing with that gracious poet of our own time, as he walked "at sunset in a time of sorrow with the Muse in her garden of thought," I think we may discover something true, or like the truth, in this his word: [1]

> Verily by beauty is it that we come at Wisdom,
> Yet not by Reason at Beauty . . .
> Here break I off,
> For not the Muse herself can tell of Goddes love;
> Which cometh to the child from the Mother's embrace,
> An Idea spacious as the starry firmament's
> Inescapable infinity of radiant gaze
> That fadeth only as it surpasseth mortal sight.

---

[1] *Testament of Beauty*, iv, 1305 ff. and 1314 ff.

THE MUSES AND THE GIFT OF HAPPINESS

"What's the goodest thing you can do?" a little girl once asked her father, the late Sir Walter Raleigh, a great lover both of children and of poetry. "Oh, I don't know. Put your hands together and say a hymn." "I think," said the child, "the goodest thing you can do is to be happy." [1]

So did Aristotle, but alas! his definition cuts out children. He defined, of course. Philosophers will do it. What, he asked, is the true function of a human being? [2] Not feeding, growing: plants and animals do that. Not feeling, not the life of mere sensation: horses, cattle, and indeed all animals share that. No, what we have to look for is the Good of Man; and that appears to be the active, reasonable (or not unreasonable) exercise of the soul's faculties, in accordance with "virtue," or "excellence"; and, if there be several human excellences, in accordance with the best, the most perfect of them. "A rough sketch," Aristotle adds, "in a department where we must not look for mathematical exactness . . . We must press on, undistracted by side issues, and, as far as

---

[1] *Letters of Sir Walter Raleigh*, ed. Lady Raleigh, vol. ii, p. 34.
[2] *Nichomachean Ethics*, i, vii, 9–16 and viii, 14.

187

possible, get clear about first principles." Finally, after a shrewd analysis of popular opinion, he arrives at this: "Happiness, then, is of all things the best, noblest, fairest, pleasantest. These qualities are not separate, as the inscription in the portico of Leto's shrine at Delos makes them:

> Justice is noblest, fairest, and health best,
> But to achieve the heart's desire is pleasantest."

The statesman's task, adds our philosopher, is to promote true Happiness, as thus defined, by helping citizens to be good people, capable of actions good and beautiful. All other goods must be regarded as conditions of such happiness, or subsidiary means to its attainment.

How admirably sane is this, compared with many doctrines preached and practised nowadays. And yet, when Aristotle tells us, "Happiness depends on the best exercise of all our best powers in a full life, both of thought and action," he is forced to the conclusion, "Children can't be happy, save by way of promise." They are far too young to think and do the sort of thing required. It seems a pity. Some of us prefer the simpler, not less searching word from Galilee: "Whosoever shall not receive the Kingdom as a little child, he shall not enter," or even that tragic word of Hecuba, once Queen of Troy: [1]

> How are we come to nothing, all our pride
> Vaded and vanished . . . What is happiness?
> One little day of living without sorrow.

---

[1] Euripides, *Hecuba*, 622 f., 627 f.; 585–592 and 684–687.

The Euripidean heroine is almost overwhelmed by an extremity of sorrow, but is saved from madness (though saved only for a moment) by the thought of a child's exquisite serenity and courage:

> Daughter, I know not of my many griefs
> Which I should contemplate. I think of one,
> Another will not let me. Grief to grief
> Succeeds, and sorrow still distracts from sorrow.
> But this that they have told me—though I weep:
> I cannot so forget as not to weep—
> Yet you have robbed grief of its sting, because
> They tell me, you were noble . . .

Hecuba's story, as Euripides presents it, ends, we know, with scenes of horror which remind us more of Webster than of Sophocles or Shakespeare. When the body of her son is shown her, murdered and mutilated by the man she trusted as a friend, she fights for sanity in vain.

> My child! My child!
> I am lost, quite lost. I am no longer I.
> What fiend of vengeance maddens me? Child, child!
> What means this frenzied strain, when I should sing thy dirge?

Almost, we seem to hear the voice of Webster's heroine:

> My soul, like to a ship in a black storm,
> Is driven, I know not whither . . .

Brightness falls from the air. Even the price of love is pain. Life is at best a mixture of grief, cruelty and ugliness, as well as beauty, joy and pity; of gross stupidity, as well as fitful vision. As Robert Bridges wrote in his old age— [1]

> We sail a changeful sea through halcyon days and storm,
> And when the ship laboureth, our steadfast purpose

---

[1] *Testament of Beauty*, i, 2–5, 30–32 and 35–36.

Trembles, like the compass in a binnacle—
Our stability is but balance.

That is true, and yet one day in June the poet
came upon a place, once a fair garden, now run
wild, but lovely still, and there experienced "a
fresh visitation of a childlike wonder," as he
watched "the common flowers . . . that starred the
fine grass of the wold—

Waving in gay display their gold-heads to the sun,
Each telling of its own inconscient happiness,
Each type a faultless essence of God's will . . .
Things supreme in themselves, eternal and unnumber'd
In the unexplor'd necessities of life and love."

The poet's *Testament of Beauty* is, I think, a
clue to a better reading of life's mystery than
Aristotle's doctrine of perfection. But the mystery
remains. We live, we have to live, as pilgrims in
a twilight, and, although it may be true, as William
James has said, that "just for this experience our
nature is adapted," we fail again and yet again.
Moments of inspiration come and pass. The
stubborn, baffling facts remain. One thing seems
certain. All our planning, our technologies, our
schemes for fostering the "values" which the
jargon of our time calls "cultural," must fail, if
we ourselves once lose our zest for life, our faith
that "happiness is best," that beauty matters.

Not long ago Mr. John Masefield wrote, in
war-time:[1]

At every birth of man a spirit takes
Flesh for a pilgrimage across our night.

---

[1] In his poem "Wonderings."

He comes with beauty, wisdom and delight,
And gathers sorrow, folly and misuse,
And, if not murdered, dies of our mistakes.

Might not the birth of every man be hailed
As a divine appearance, come to lead
Men to the living brotherhood they need? . . .

Might not such reverence for life prepare
A state more worth, wherein each citizen
Might have for faith the world of fellow men,
For charity a paradise on earth,
For hope the beauty of the singing there?

There are critics, I am told, who ask us to leave beauty out of all our calculation about art and even morals. Certainly beauty is incalculable. So are many things that matter more than measurable, calculable facts. These are the things the Muses understand. What Pindar wrote for a beloved young athlete more than two thousand years ago is relevant to our concerns to-day:

The spirit of youth, when his desire comes true,
Fresh, unexpected, beautiful, awakes
To manhood. Suddenly his youth has wings.
His thoughts are above riches. But, as joy
Flowers in a moment, so the untoward thought
Comes, and, as quickly, pleasure fades and falls
To the earth, wither'd. Creatures of a day—
What is a man? What not? A shadow's dream.
Yet, while a glint of sunshine visits us
From heaven, we walk in light, and honeysweet
It is, to be alive and be a man.[1]

That is a typical Greek view, and it is this, or something like it, that the Muses offer for our help throughout the long tradition both of Greek and English poetry, this recognition of the miracle of

[1] *Pythian*, viii, 88 ff.

life, of which the miracle of music and of poetry
is part, this quickened apprehension of the sudden
glory which, although it passes, and our logic
cannot prove its origin or purpose, gives the heart
a deep assurance, fairer than all proof.

> It is not growing like a tree . . . or standing like an oak . . .
>   A lily of a day
>   Is fairer far in May,
> Although it fall and die that night;
> It was the plant and flower of light.

So Ben Jonson wrote of two young gentlemen who
passed, according to our human reckoning, before
their time, but sowed the fruits of friendship and of
virtue and had got the harvest in before they went.

Could there be any better answer to the little
girl who asked, "What's the goodest thing you
can do?" than the lines her father left us?[1]

> Though our songs
> Cannot vanquish ancient wrongs,
> Though they follow where the rose
>   Goes;
>
> And their sound,
> Swooning over hollow ground,
> Fade and leave the enchanted air
>   Bare;
>
> Yet the wise
> Say that not unblest he dies
> Who has known a single May
>   Day.
>
> If we have laughed,
> Loved, and laboured in our craft,
> We may pass with a resigned
>   Mind.

---

[1] From Walter Raleigh's "Ode to the Glasgow Ballad Club, 21st
Dec. 1901," published in *Laughter from a Cloud* (Constable), 1922.